logolounge

2,000 International Identities by Leading Designers

GLOUCESTER MASSACHUSETTS

ROCKPORT PUBLISHERS

Bill Gardner and Catharine Fishel

First published in the United States of America by
Rockport Publishers, a member of
Quayside Publishing Group
33 Commercial Street
Gloucester, Massachusetts 01930-5089
Telephone: (978) 282-9590
Fax: (978) 283-2742
www.rockpub.com

ISBN 1-59253-224-1

10 9 8 7 6 5 4 3 2

Design: Gardner Design
Layout & Production: *tabula rasa* graphic design
Cover Image: Gardner Design

Printed in China

contents

introduction

When LogoLounge.com first went online in late 2001, we had no idea how enthusiastic a response we would receive from some of the design industry's most talented and prolific designers. A who's who of designers from six continents began uploading thousands of logos to the website, and they continue to do so today. Lesser-known but still exciting individuals and firms have also come on board, adding even more depth and breadth to the collection.

As this enormous resource began to gel, the logical next step seemed to be an annual—a printed companion—that would assemble the best and most exciting work from the site each year. But rather than just produce a one-dimensional collection without context, we decided to create a book with (a) substantial content, and (b) a companion website that allows you to search the book's contents. Simply log onto www.logolounge.com/book1, and you will be able to swiftly navigate through the more than two thousand logos in this book by searching by designer, client, industry, type of logo, or keywords.

A panel of nine renowned identity designers from around the globe selected this collection. Their choices form an inspirational resource and reference tool through which you can explore the trends and influences driving international branding today. In the book and on the companion website, the logos have been arranged categorically to allow for fast access and to show off the dramatic diversity of styles used to depict similar subject matter.

Our goal is to inspire and educate you without exhausting you (or your supply of sticky notes) in the process. LogoLounge.com and this volume are truly hybrids of print and Web: You may read at your leisure, or do a quick, intuitive search. Our sincere hope is that *LogoLounge* will open up more time for you to do what you like best: design.

—Bill Gardner and Cathy Fishel

Sean Adams
AdamsMorioka, Inc.,
Los Angeles, CA

Mexican Doorbell logo,
by Art Chantry

"How can you resist a logo with a dead dog? I loved this because it was unexpected, smart, and perfectly executed. The hand-drawn quality gave it a vitality and immediacy that a hard-line, smooth mark would have missed."

Noreen Morioka
AdamsMorioka,
Los Angeles, CA

Dracula logo,
by Chase Design Group

"I'm always a sucker for logos that evoke an emotional response in a concise and poignant way. I tend to like the humorous more than the serious, but this logo is one that provokes an immediate response and narrative. I wish that more entertainment work could be as wonderfully refined and memorable."

In 1993, Sean Adams and Noreen Morioka founded AdamsMorioka with the idea of applying clarity, purity, and resonance to content, form, and business. The duo has been named to the ID40 list, *I.D. Magazine*'s annual list of the forty most influential international designers. Both have lectured around the world, have been nominated for the National Design Award, and are Fellows of the International Design Competition at Aspen. They also frequently serve as jurors for leading competitions.

Adams is past president of the Los Angeles chapter of the American Institute of Graphic Arts (AIGA-LA) and has served on AIGA's National Board. He teaches design theory and typography at the California Institute of the Arts.

Mary Lewis
Lewis Moberly,
London, UK

*National Association for Child
Development and Education
logo, by Pat Taylor Inc.*
*"I chose the symbol for the asso-
ciation because it said a great
deal in a very edited way. Two
heads linked by an arm, or two
eyes and a smile, is an intriguing
image that creates a powerful,
emotive communication."*

Mary Lewis, creative director of
Lewis Moberly, has won numerous design awards, including the
industry's highly prestigious
British Design and Art Direction
Award for Outstanding Design
and the Design Business Association International Design Effec-
tiveness Awards Grand Prix. She
has chaired the BBC Graphic
Design Awards, is a past president of British Design and Art
Direction, and is a member of
the Royal Mail Stamps Advisory
Committee. In 2001, Lewis
received the British Design and
Art Direction President's Award
for Outstanding Achievement.

She speaks to groups around
the world and has participated
in such prestigious gatherings
as Leaders in Design, a series
of creative workshops initiated
by Prime Minister Tony Blair.
Lewis also coauthored the book
Understanding Brands.

Rex Peteet
Sibley/Peteet Design,
Dallas, TX

Elisabeth Andersen logo, by Jon Flaming Design

"The mark has an unstudied spontaneity about it. It is very gestural, so it doesn't stand still—ideal for women's fashion. I am uncertain of the inspiration, but it reminds me of the famous photograph of Marilyn Monroe standing on the subway grate, dress billowing. All of the information you need is there with a few very ingenious shapes. The attitude and arms are implied with negative space and body gesture. So, with no unnecessary elements, the designer captures the free-spirited loveliness and elegance of this woman and leaves just enough to the viewer's own imagination."

After studying design at the University of North Texas, Rex Peteet worked with several prestigious firms, including The Richards Group and Pirtle Design. Twenty years ago, he and partner Don Sibley founded their own company, Sibley/Peteet Design, in Dallas. In 1994, Peteet founded the firm's second office in Austin, where he now lives and works.

He has won numerous regional and national design awards, and his work is frequently published in international design periodicals and annuals; it is also represented in the permanent collection of the Library of Congress. Peteet serves on the advisory boards of AIGA-Austin and the Creative Circus Design School in Atlanta. He also judges, lectures, and teaches seminars for universities and design organizations across the country.

Woody Pirtle
New York, NY

TiVo logo, by the Cronan Group
"I love the honesty and approach-
ability of the TiVo logo. In an arena
of planets, globes, rings, shooting
stars, swooshes, and every other
cosmic gewgaw being used to
identify some gadget or service
in our new digital world, TiVo is a
breath of fresh air."

After running his own successful design practice in Dallas for ten years, Woody Pirtle joined Penta-gram in New York in 1988. He is well known for his economical logotypes and witty posters, and his identity and publication design work perennially put him at the top of lists of awards and most-wanted speakers. His work is exhibited worldwide and is in the permanent collections of many museums, including the Museum of Modern Art, the Cooper-Hewitt Museum, and the Zurich Poster Museum.

Marcel Robbers
Braue; Branding and
Corporate Design,
Bremerhaven, Germany

New England Patriots logo,
by Evenson Design Group
"Simplicity, use of color, strength,
a clear message, dynamism, and
longevity are the key elements of
the logo in my point of view. The
simplicity in the different ele-
ments works together perfectly
with the colors, and thus creates
the logo's overall bold appear-
ance. It has the strength and abil-
ity to convey a clear message
even when the text isn't added."

Marcel Robbers is art director of
Braue, a company specializing in
branding and corporate design
that was founded by his boyhood
friend, Kai Braue. His unique
solutions have helped his many
international clients build and
strengthen their brands. Robbers'
work in logos and corporate
identity has been published in
many graphic design magazines
and books in Germany and
abroad, and he has received
numerous awards. In his spare
time, Robbers is the renowned
singer for his heavy metal band,
2nd Heat.

Felix Sockwell

Felixsockwell.com,
New York, NY

National Museum of Australia logo, by SPATCHURST

"It's great to be smart, to nail a logo into its name or function. But over the years, I've learned it's better to be brave—to craft something from the heart. God walked into the room when this one was handed out. It could be for anything, but somehow only feels right in Australia."

Felix Sockwell is a Texas native. He cut his teeth designing logos for friends after work. Barbecue sauces, restaurants, bars, five hair salons—everyone lined up for his famous free logos. It got so bad, he says, that coworkers nick-named him "FREElix" and threw change into his office. Eventually, however, awards and attention arrived, and he moved from Dallas to San Francisco and then to New York, where he founded what is now the Brand Integration Group at Ogilvy & Mather. He left the agency after creating a number of large identity programs and became an illustrator in the summer of 1999. Since then, he has built a strong reputation in the field of identity design.

Peter Watts
Watts Design, Melbourne,
Australia

*Frenchbread Productions logo,
by Dotzero Design*
"Simplicity, nice colors, and a
campaignable idea all combine for
a memorable and emotive logo."

Graphic design has been a life-long passion for Peter Watts, founder of Watts Design. He has embraced an extensive range of design disciplines, including packaging, annual reports, corporate communication, environmental design, and corporate identity. His strong commitment to quality and innovation consistently puts his communication solutions at the forefront of trends, where they win awards and publication in annuals around the world.

Ann Willoughby
Willoughby Design Group,
Kansas City, MO

*Richmond Raceway logo, by
Gardner Design*
"I always appreciate simple solutions that work on many levels. The racetrack and the double Rs make for a playful visual palindrome. Great color, too."

Ann Willoughby is the founding partner and creative director of Willoughby Design, formed in 1978. Willoughby provides strategic oversight for Fortune 500 companies as well as brand start-ups. She and her seventeen associates specialize in retail brand identity and brand communications, and Willoughby also frequently lectures to design, education, and business groups. She has served on the advisory board of the Kansas City AIGA and is currently on the steering committee of the national AIGA Brand Design group. Teaching is one of her passions, and she works with students and children whenever possible. She and her firm have won a number of industry awards and had their work published in many leading design publications.

Initials

	A	B

Ⓓ = Design Firm   Ⓒ = Client

1A Ⓓ Planet Propaganda Ⓒ Adams Outdoor Advertising   1B Ⓓ Planet Propaganda Ⓒ Adams Outdoor Advertising
2A Ⓓ Wages Design Ⓒ Atlanta Flames Hockey   2B Ⓓ Balance Ⓒ Atlas Oil
3A Ⓓ Hornall Anderson Ⓒ Aiki Bakery   3B Ⓓ Rickabaugh Graphics Ⓒ Atlas Color Imaging

14

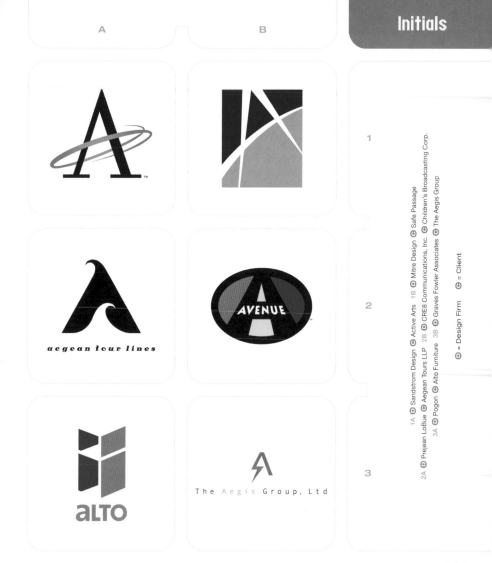

A B

1

2

3

1A ⒹSandstrom Design ⒸActive Arts 1B ⒹMitre Design ⒸSafe Passage
2A ⒹPrejean LoBue ⒸAegean Tours LLP 2B ⒹCRE8 Communications, Inc. ⒸChildren's Broadcasting Corp.
3A ⒹPogon ⒸAlto Furniture 3B ⒹGraves Fowler Associates ⒸThe Aegis Group

Ⓓ = Design Firm Ⓒ = Client

A

B

1

2

3

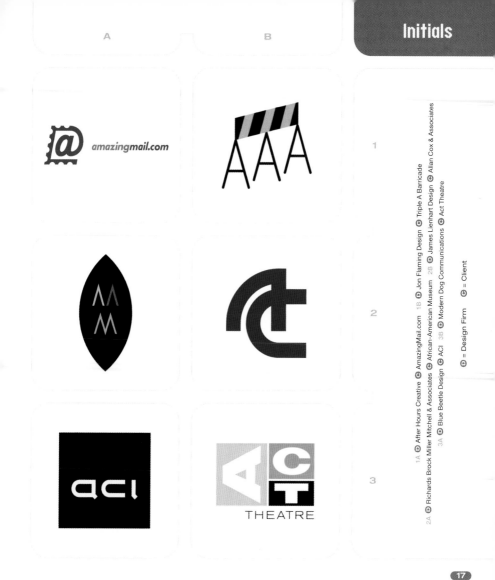

A

B

1

2

3

1A Ⓓ After Hours Creative Ⓒ AmazingMail.com 1B Ⓓ Jon Flaming Design Ⓒ Triple A Barricade

2A Ⓓ Richards Brock Miller Mitchell & Associates Ⓒ African-American Museum 2B Ⓓ James Lienhart Design Ⓒ Allan Cox & Associates

3A Ⓓ Blue Beetle Design Ⓒ ACI 3B Ⓓ Modern Dog Communications Ⓒ Act Theatre

Ⓓ = Design Firm   Ⓒ = Client

1A Ⓓ Randy Mosher Design Ⓒ Three Floyds, LLC 1B Ⓓ Howalt Design Studio, Inc. Ⓒ Benedictine High School
2A Ⓓ Pat Taylor Inc. Ⓒ Berstrom Museum 2B Ⓓ Chase Design Group Ⓒ Bradley Group
3A Ⓓ Pogon Ⓒ Bastion Shipping 3B Ⓓ Prejean LoBue Ⓒ Corporate Concepts - PBS

Ⓓ = Design Firm   Ⓒ = Client

A

B

ⓓ = Design Firm   ⓒ = Client

1A ⓓ Eisenberg and Associates ⓒ Bella Corium 1B ⓓ Kiku Obata & Company ⓒ Brown Shoe
2A ⓓ Howalt Design Studio, Inc. ⓒ Blackstone 2B ⓓ Howalt Design Studio, Inc. ⓒ Blackstone
3A ⓓ Planet Propaganda ⓒ Sherpa 3B ⓓ Design and Image ⓒ Blueline

1

2

3

BROWN SHOE

BLACKSTONE

BLACKSTONE

BLUELINE
BUILDING SERVICES INC

1

2

3

1A ⒟ Stone & Ward ⒞ Marketplace Grill   1B ⒟ Chermayeff & Geismar Inc.   ⒞ Beaunit
2A ⒟ Hornall Anderson ⒞ Blue Nile   2B ⒟ Hutchinson Associates, Inc.   ⒞ BRX
3A ⒟ Trickett & Webb ⒞ European Science Foundation   3B ⒟ feluxe ⒞ none—for sale

⒟ = Design Firm   ⒞ = Client

21

⊕ = Design Firm   ⊖ = Client

1A ⊕ Richards Brock Miller Mitchell & Associates ⊖ Circuits 1B ⊕ Jon Flaming Design ⊖ Creative Printing

2A ⊕ CRE8 Communications, Inc. ⊖ The Certus Group 2B ⊕ Sayles Graphic Design, Inc. ⊖ Christopher's Restaurant

3A ⊕ Pat Taylor Inc. ⊖ Commons Corporate Center 3B ⊕ Gardner Design ⊖ Christy Peters

A   B

1

2

3

A

B

CURRENT COMMUNICATIONS

C N E T

CLC ASSOCIATES

Carlson West Povondra **Architects**

1

2

3

1A ⒹPrejean LoBue ⒸCNET Telecommunications 1B ⒹSabingrafik, Inc. ⒸCurrent Communications
2A ⒹChermayeff & Geismar Inc. ⒸCentro de Convenciones de Cartagena 2B ⒹBraue; Branding & Corporate Design ⒸSony - Columbia Records
3A ⒹDesign and Image ⒸCLC Associates 3B ⒹWebster Design Associates Inc. ⒸCarlson West Pavondra Architects

Ⓓ = Design Firm   Ⓒ = Client

23

Initials

D = Design Firm **C** = Client

A   B

1

2

3

1A **D** SPATCHURST **C** Digital Art Directory 1B **D** Richards Brock Miller Mitchell & Associates **C** Dallas Symphony Orchestra
2A **D** Chermayeff & Geismar Inc. **C** Demir Dokum 2B **D** Chermayeff & Geismar Inc. **C** D-Day National Museum
3A **D** Gardner Design **C** Diehlvolk Furniture 3B **D** James Lienhart Design **C** Dunbar Builders

24

A   B

1

2

3

1A ⊙ Design Machine ⊙ Design Machine   1B ⊙ Beth Singer Design ⊙ Democratic National Committee

2A ⊙ Dotzero Design ⊙ Digital Planet   2B ⊙ Planet Propaganda ⊙ EuroArte

3A ⊙ Rickabaugh Graphics ⊙ Beckett Paper   3B ⊙ Chermayeff & Geismar Inc. ⊙ Engraved Stationary Manufacturers Association

⊙ = Design Firm   ⊙ = Client

25

A

B

1

2

3

Ⓓ = Design Firm　Ⓒ = Client

1A Ⓓ Hornall Anderson Ⓒ Elseware Corporation　1B Ⓓ Pat Taylor Inc. Ⓒ Frank Evans Art Supplies

2A Ⓓ Grapefruit Design Ⓒ Media Engine　2B Ⓓ Bumba Design Ⓒ Estess Music Management and Entertainment

3A Ⓓ Miriello Grafico, Inc. Ⓒ Encorrot Sportswear　3B Ⓓ Sanna Design Group, Inc. Ⓒ Orange E - Graphic

eLustro
Agendas

ESTES
entertainment

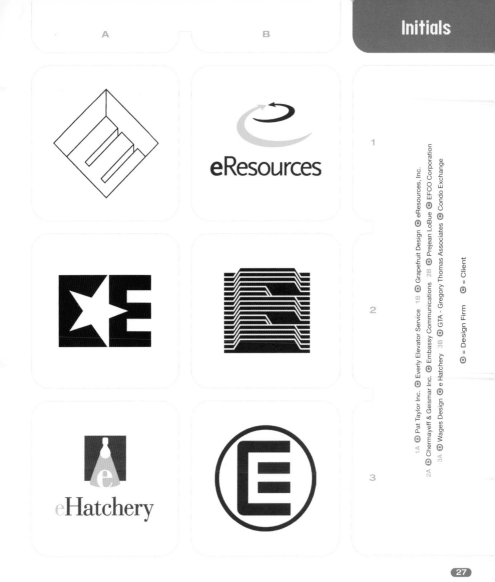

A   B

Initials

eResources

eHatchery

1

2

3

1A ⓓ Pat Taylor Inc. ⓒ Everly Elevator Service   1B ⓓ Grapefruit Design ⓒ eResources, Inc.

2A ⓓ Chermayeff & Geismar Inc. ⓒ Embassy Communications   2B ⓓ Prejean LoBue ⓒ EFCO Corporation

3A ⓓ Wages Design ⓒ e Hatchery   3B ⓓ GTA - Gregory Thomas Associates ⓒ Condo Exchange

ⓓ = Design Firm   ⓒ = Client

27

D = Design Firm   **C** = Client

1A **D** Hornall Anderson **C** Microsoft Corporation   1B **D** Cato Purnell Partners **C** Eden Quarter
2A **D** John Evans Design **C** Squires and Co.   2B **D** Sandstrom Design **C** FSU
3A **D** Simon & Goetz Design **C** FX Schmidt Spiele   3B **D** Gardner Design **C** Lazy G Ranch

1

2

3

A

B

GEUS

DANMARKS OG GRØNLANDS GEOLOGISKE UNDERSØGELSE
MILJØ- OG ENERGIMINISTERIET

grow

GCG FINANCIAL

General
Cinema

1

2

3

1A Ⓓ Kontrapunkt Ⓒ The Geological Survey of Denmark and Greenland 1B Ⓓ Liska + Associates Communication Design Ⓒ Geldermann

2A Ⓓ Simon & Goetz Design Ⓒ Grow 2B Ⓓ Grapefruit Design Ⓒ Boston Media Corporation

3A Ⓓ Liska + Associates Communication Design Ⓒ GCG Financial 3B Ⓓ BrandEquity Ⓒ General Cinema Corporation

Ⓓ = Design Firm   Ⓒ = Client

	A	B

1

g:f
graves fowler associates

2

GORSUCH KIRGIS

GSD&M

3

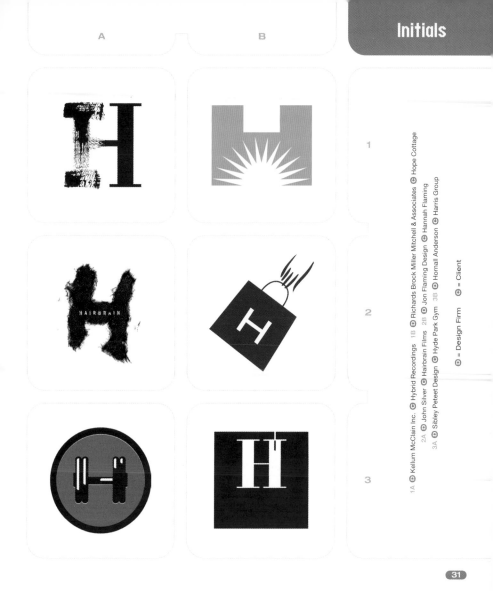

1

2

3

1A Ⓓ Kellum McClain Inc. Ⓒ Hybrid Recordings   1B Ⓓ Richards Brock Miller Mitchell & Associates Ⓒ Hope Cottage

2A Ⓓ John Silver Ⓒ Hairbrain Films   2B Ⓓ Jon Flaming Design Ⓒ Hannah Flaming

3A Ⓓ Sibley Peteet Design Ⓒ Hyde Park Gym   3B Ⓓ Hornall Anderson Ⓒ Harris Group

Ⓓ = Design Firm   Ⓒ = Client

A

B

1

2

3

Ⓓ = Design Firm   Ⓒ = Client

1A Ⓓ Liska + Associates Communication Design Ⓒ Heltzer, Inc.   1B Ⓓ Hornall Anderson Ⓒ Hardware.com

2A Ⓓ Wages Design Ⓒ Hardin Construction   2B Ⓓ Balance Ⓒ Humaneered

3A Ⓓ Planet Propaganda Ⓒ The Hiebing Group   3B Ⓓ MB Design Ⓒ Hotel Bellwether

A

B

1

2

3

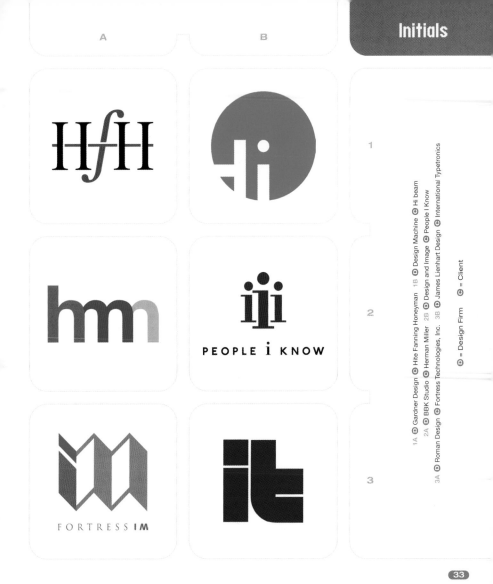

FORTRESS **IM**

PEOPLE **I** KNOW

1A Ⓓ Gardner Design ⒸHite Fanning Honeyman   1B ⒹDesign Machine ⒸHi beam
2A ⒹBBK Studio ⒸHerman Miller   2B ⒹDesign and Image ⒸPeople I Know
3A ⒹRoman Design ⒸFortress Technologies, Inc.   3B ⒹJames Lienhart Design ⒸInternational Typetronics

Ⓓ = Design Firm   Ⓒ = Client

33

Initials

A   **B**

1   **2**   **3**

D = Design Firm   **C** = Client

1A **D** Design Machine **C** L2   1B **D** MB Design **C** James Alan Salon

2A **D** Chermayeff & Geismar Inc. **C** Krystal   2B **D** Gardner Design **C** Kimball Insurance

3A **D** Chase Design Group **C** Kemper Snowboards   3B **D** Saturn Flyer **C** KRYPTOSIMA

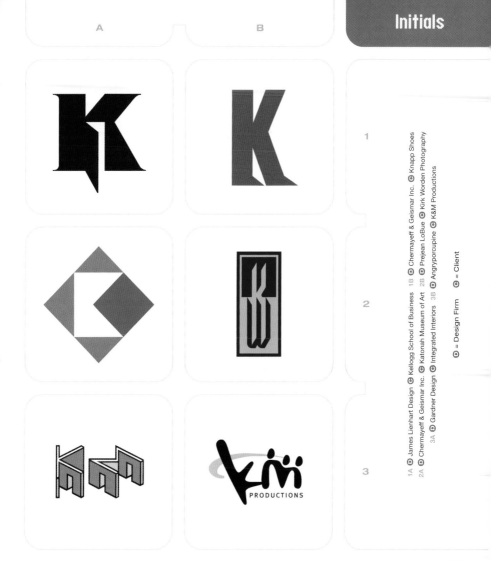

A

B

1

2

3

1A **D** James Lienhart Design **C** Kellogg School of Business 1B **D** Chermayeff & Geismar Inc. **C** Knapp Shoes

2A **D** Chermayeff & Geismar Inc. **C** Katonah Museum of Art 2B **D** Prejean LoBue **C** Kirk Worden Photography

3A **D** Gardner Design **C** Integrated Interiors 3B **D** Angryporcupine **C** K&M Productions

D = Design Firm   **C** = Client

PRODUCTIONS

A

B

1

2

3

A

B

Initials

1

2

3

LISA ERSHIG INTERIORS

MARKET

McCORD PRINTING

1A **D** MB Design **C** Lisa Ershig Interiors 1B **D** Pat Taylor Inc. **C** Magna-Check Corporation
2A **D** Howalt Design Studio, Inc. **C** Market Skateboards 2B **D** Prejean LoBue **C** Linda & Manuel Herrera
3A **D** Eisenberg and Associates **C** McCord Printing 3B **D** Dennis Purcell Design **C** Manitou, Inc.

D = Design Firm   **C** = Client

37

A

B

1

2

3

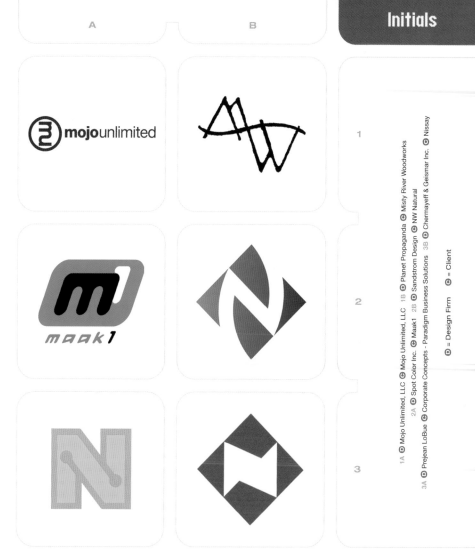

A

B

1

2

3

1A ⒟ Mojo Unlimited, LLC ⒞ Mojo Unlimited, LLC 1B ⒟ Planet Propaganda ⒞ Misty River Woodworks

2A ⒟ Spot Color Inc. ⒞ Maak1 2B ⒟ Sandstrom Design ⒞ NW Natural

3A ⒟ Prejean LoBue ⒞ Corporate Concepts - Paradigm Business Solutions 3B ⒟ Chermayeff & Geismar Inc. ⒞ Nissay

⒟ = Design Firm   ⒞ = Client

ⓓ = Design Firm   ⓒ = Client

1A ⓓ Howalt Design Studio, Inc. ⓒ Net Trekker   1B ⓓ Liska + Associates Communication Design ⓒ Northwestern Nasal + Sinus
2A ⓓ Chermayeff & Geismar Inc. ⓒ National Public Radio   2B ⓓ Henderson Bromstead Art Co. ⓒ Nupro
3A ⓓ Pogon ⓒ Only   3B ⓓ Rickabaugh Graphics ⓒ Ohio State University

1

2

3

net trekker

NN
NORTHWESTERN NASAL + SINUS

ONLY
MEGASTORE

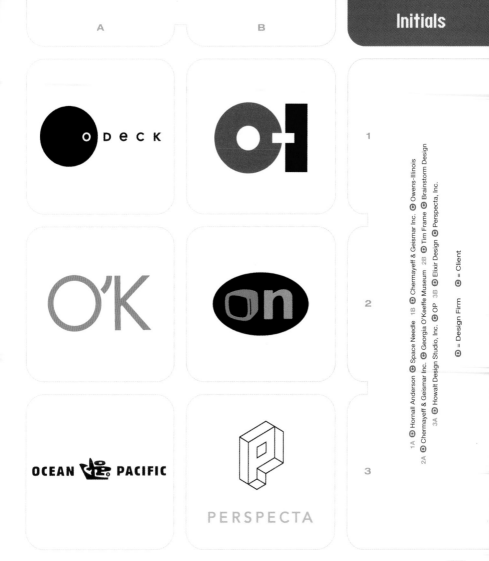

1

2

3

1A **D** Hornall Anderson **C** Space Needle 1B **D** Chermayeff & Geismar Inc. **C** Owens-Illinois

2A **D** Chermayeff & Geismar Inc. **C** Georgia O'Keeffe Museum 2B **D** Tim Frame **C** Brainstorm Design

3A **D** Howalt Design Studio, Inc. **C** OP 3B **D** Elixir Design **C** Perspecta, Inc.

D = Design Firm   **C** = Client

A

B

1

2

3

Ⓓ = Design Firm   Ⓒ = Client

1A Ⓓ Planet Propaganda Ⓒ Planet Propaganda 1B Ⓓ Gardner Design Ⓒ PrintMaster Printing
2A Ⓓ Planet Propaganda Ⓒ Planet Design Company 2B Ⓓ Wages Design Ⓒ Pfrimmer
3A Ⓓ Sibley Peteet Design Ⓒ Paramount Theater 3B Ⓓ Howalt Design Studio, Inc. Ⓒ Palm

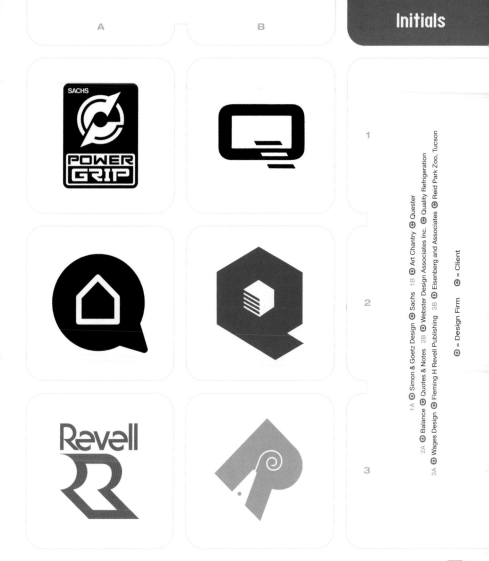

1A ⒟ Simon & Goetz Design ⒞ Sachs   1B ⒟ Art Chantry ⒞ Quester

2A ⒟ Balance ⒞ Quotes & Notes   2B ⒟ Webster Design Associates Inc. ⒞ Quality Refrigeration

3A ⒟ Wages Design ⒞ Fleming H Revell Publishing   3B ⒟ Eisenberg and Associates ⒞ Reid Park Zoo, Tucson

⒟ = Design Firm   ⒞ = Client

A

B

1

2

3

D = Design Firm   **C** = Client

1A **D** Evenson Design Group **C** Reading Entertainment   1B **D** Dotzero Design **C** Rich Henderson

2A **D** Pat Taylor Inc. **C** Bill Rolle & Associates   2B **D** Hornall Anderson **C** Pacific Raceways

3A **D** Liska + Associates Communication Design **C** Racine Art Museum (RAM)   3B **D** Chermayeff & Geismar Inc. **C** Robert F. Kennedy Foundation

	A	B
1		
2	SPORT SPECIFIC FITNESS	
3		SATER, INC. PUNCH | BEND | WELD

1A **D** Gardner Design **C** Richmond Raceway 1B **D** Braue: Branding & Corporate Design **C** Rilke & Sandelmann Fotografen

2A **D** Treehouse Design **C** Sport Specific Fitness by Christopher Drozd 2B **D** Gardner Design **C** Shelton Collision Repair

3A **D** John Evans Design **C** Jeff Stephens 3B **D** Tim Frame **C** Sater, Inc.

D = Design Firm **C** = Client

45

A

B

1

2

3

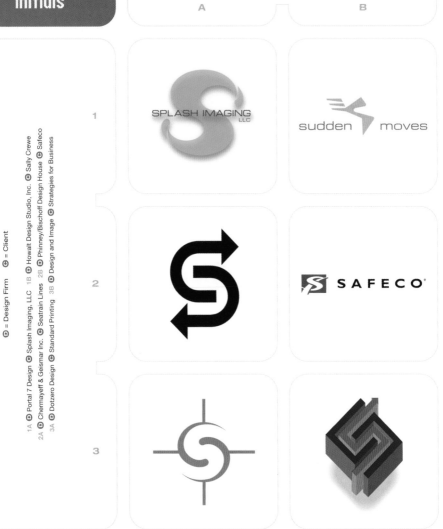

D = Design Firm   **C** = Client

1A **D** Portal 7 Design **C** Splash Imaging, LLC   1B **D** Howalt Design Studio, Inc. **C** Sally Crewe
2A **D** Chermayeff & Geismar Inc. **C** Seatrain Lines   2B **D** Phinney/Bischoff Design House **C** Safeco
3A **D** Dotzero Design **C** Standard Printing   3B **D** Design and Image **C** Strategies for Business

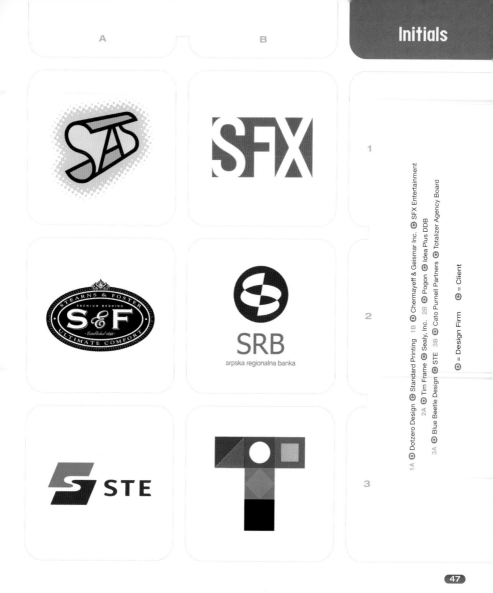

1

2

3

1A ⑩ Dotzero Design ⑥ Standard Printing 1B ⑩ Chermayeff & Geismar Inc. ⑥ SFX Entertainment

2A ⑩ Tim Frame ⑥ Sealy, Inc. 2B ⑩ Pogon ⑥ Idea Plus DDB

3A ⑩ Blue Beetle Design ⑥ STE 3B ⑩ Cato Purnell Partners ⑥ Totalizer Agency Board

⑩ = Design Firm   ⑥ = Client

srpska regionalna banka

STE

A

B

1

2

3

Ⓓ = Design Firm   Ⓒ = Client

1A Ⓓ Hornall Anderson Ⓒ Raleigh Cycle Company of America   1B Ⓓ Design and Image Ⓒ Timberline Industries
2A Ⓓ Tharp Did It Ⓒ Temple   2B Ⓓ Sandstrom Design Ⓒ Thurber Works
3A Ⓓ SPATCHURST Ⓒ Tomago Aluminium   3B Ⓓ Chermayeff & Geismar Inc. Ⓒ Telemundo

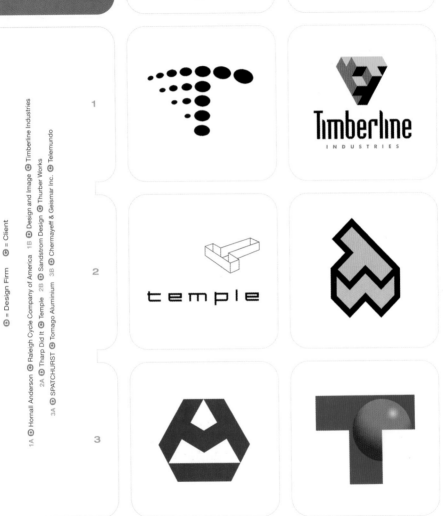

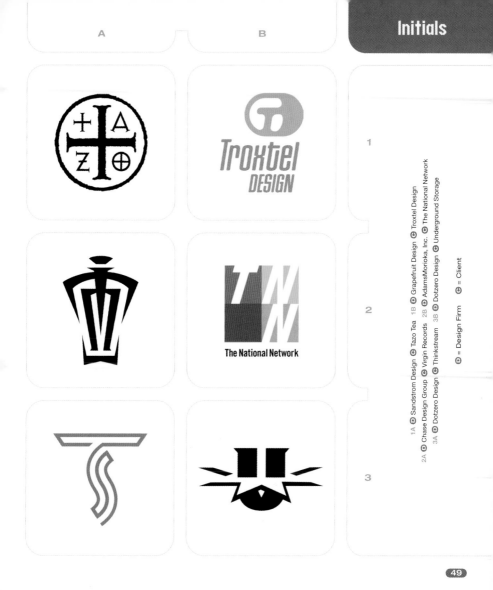

	A	B
1		
2		
3		

1A **D** Sandstrom Design **C** Tazo Tea 1B **D** Grapefruit Design **C** Troxtel Design

2A **D** Chase Design Group **C** Virgin Records 2B **D** AdamsMorioka, Inc. **C** The National Network

3A **D** Dotzero Design **C** Thinkstream 3B **D** Dotzero Design **C** Underground Storage

D = Design Firm **C** = Client

A B

1

Universal Health Network

2

V I S T A
s y s t e m s

3

🅓 = Design Firm 🅒 = Client

1A 🅓 John Silver 🅒 Peter Geiss 1B 🅓 GTA - Gregory Thomas Associates 🅒 Universal Health Network
2A 🅓 Richards Brock Miller Mitchell & Associates 🅒 USA Film Festival 2B 🅓 Design One 🅒 Vista Systems
3A 🅓 Cato Purnell Partners 🅒 Australian Symphony Orchestra 3B 🅓 Braue; Branding & Corporate Design 🅒 Braue

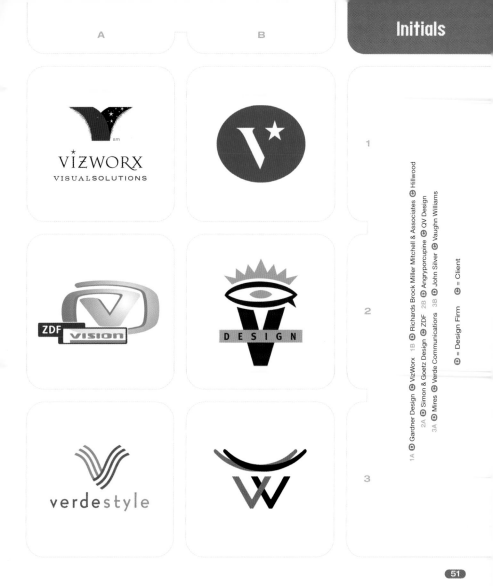

A

B

1

2

3

1A ⓓ Gardner Design ⓒ VizWorx   1B ⓓ Richards Brock Miller Mitchell & Associates ⓒ Hillwood
2A ⓓ Simon & Goetz Design ⓒ ZDF   2B ⓓ Angryporcupine ⓒ QV Design
3A ⓓ Mires ⓒ Verde Communications   3B ⓓ John Silver ⓒ Vaughn Williams

ⓓ = Design Firm   ⓒ = Client

A

B

Ⓓ = Design Firm   Ⓒ = Client

1A Ⓓ Cato Purnell Partners Ⓒ Bank West   1B Ⓓ Hornall Anderson Ⓒ Watson Furniture Company
2A Ⓓ Howalt Design Studio, Inc. Ⓒ Winternet   2B Ⓓ Mongile Associates Inc. Ⓒ Winterthur Museum, Garden, and Library
3A Ⓓ Hornall Anderson Ⓒ Widmer Brothers Brewery   3B Ⓓ Blue Beetle Design Ⓒ Wood Smith

1

2

3

	A	B
1		
2		
3		

1A ⒟ Howalt Design Studio, Inc. ⒞ Work, Inc.   1B ⒟ Evenson Design Group ⒞ Waldorf Crawford

2A ⒟ CRE8 Communications, Inc. ⒞ Western Recreational Vehicles, Inc.   2B ⒟ Henderson Bromstead Art Co. ⒞ Winston–Salem Symphony

3A ⒟ Design and Image ⒞ Wewatta Transfer   3B ⒟ Chase Design Group ⒞ Tony Williams

⒟ = Design Firm   ⒞ = Client

D = Design Firm   **C** = Client

1A **D** Chermayeff & Geismar Inc. **C** Waterside   1B **D** DK Design **C** Six Flags Magic Mountain
2A **D** Sterling Group **C** Exenet   2B **D** After Hours Creative **C** ENX
3A **D** Simon & Goetz Design **C** Yarell GmbH   3B **D** Sibley Peteet Design **C** Yancy's Bar

1

2

3

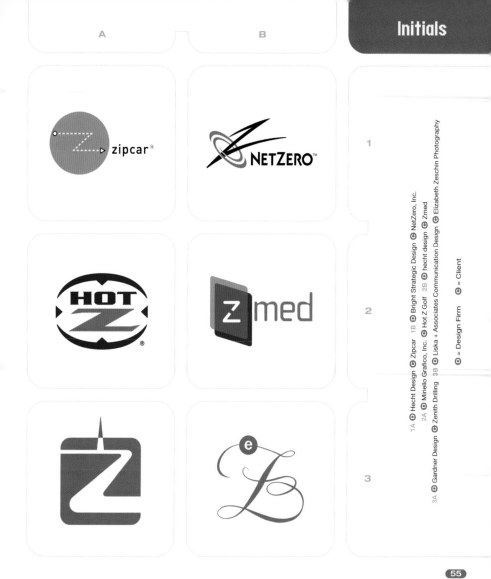

1

2

3

1A ⓓ Hecht Design ⓒ Zipcar 1B ⓓ Bright Strategic Design ⓒ NetZero, Inc.

2A ⓓ Miriello Grafico, Inc. ⓒ Hot Z Golf 2B ⓓ hecht design ⓒ Zmed

3A ⓓ Gardner Design ⓒ Zenith Drilling 3B ⓓ Liska + Associates Communication Design ⓒ Elizabeth Zeschin Photography

ⓓ = Design Firm   ⓒ = Client

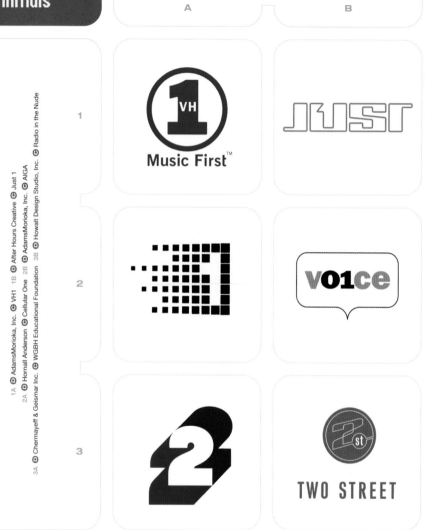

D = Design Firm   **C** = Client

1A **D** AdamsMorioka, Inc. **C** VH1   1B **D** After Hours Creative **C** Just 1
2A **D** Hornall Anderson **C** Cellular One   2B **D** AdamsMorioka, Inc. **C** AIGA
3A **D** Chermayeff & Geismar Inc. **C** WGBH Educational Foundation   3B **D** Howalt Design Studio, Inc. **C** Radio in the Nude

1

2

3

A   B

1

2

3

1A ⒹHowalt Design Studio, Inc. ⒸEast3 1B ⒹCato Purnell Partners ⒸAGideas

2A ⒹSimon & Goetz Design ⒸSachs 2B ⒹMB Design ⒸHaskell Corporation

3A ⒹChermayeff & Geismar Inc. ⒸWNEV Television 3B ⒹCato Purnell Partners ⒸSeven Network Australia

Ⓓ = Design Firm   Ⓒ = Client

A

B

1

2

3

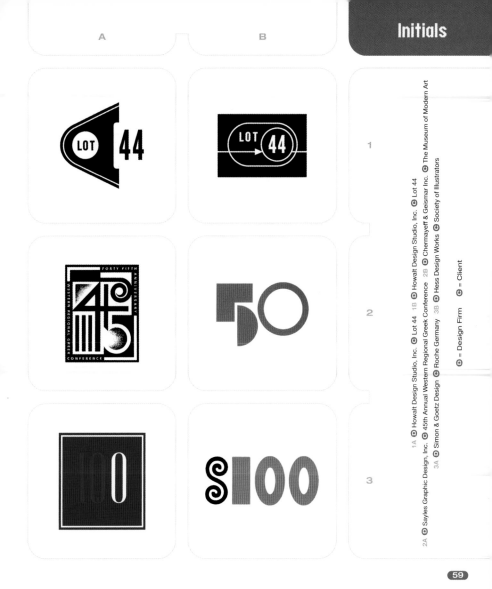

1

2

3

1A ⓓ Howalt Design Studio, Inc. ⓒ Lot 44 1B ⓓ Howalt Design Studio, Inc. ⓒ Lot 44

2A ⓓ Sayles Graphic Design, Inc. ⓒ 45th Annual Western Regional Greek Conference 2B ⓓ Chermayeff & Geismar Inc. ⓒ The Museum of Modern Art

3A ⓓ Simon & Goetz Design ⓒ Roche Germany 3B ⓓ Hess Design Works ⓒ Society of Illustrators

ⓓ = Design Firm   ⓒ = Client

A

B

1

2

3

⊕ = Design Firm   ⊛ = Client

1A ⊕ Sibley Peteet Design ⊛ McGarrah Jessee 1B ⊕ Chase Design Group ⊛ Hard Rock Hotel
2A ⊕ Felixsockwell.com ⊛ 850 2B ⊕ Lieber Cooper Associates ⊛ J.W. Marriott - Washington D.C.
3A ⊕ Design and Image ⊛ Race Street Partners 3B ⊕ Gardner Design ⊛ Grider & Company CPA

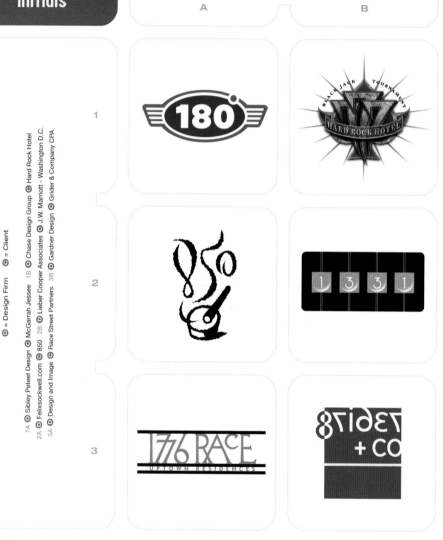

A

B

1

Filmcore

oppor2unity

2

estyle.com

kidstyle.com

babystyle.com

hi?fi
TUESDAYS

3

Bike(LIFT)™

How tight?

1A Ⓓ Sandstrom Design Ⓒ Filmcore 1B Ⓓ Kellum McClain Inc. Ⓒ Greco Ethridge Inc.
2A Ⓓ Chase Design Group Ⓒ estyle.com 2B Ⓓ Proart Graphics/Gabriel Kalach Ⓒ Joy Night Club
3A Ⓓ Sandstrom Design Ⓒ Bike Lift 3B Ⓓ Pat Taylor Inc. Ⓒ Typographers International Association

Ⓓ = Design Firm   Ⓒ = Client

A

B

1

2

3

Ⓓ = Design Firm   Ⓒ = Client

1A Ⓓ Sackett Design Ⓒ Workplace Answers   1B Ⓓ Chermayeff & Geismar Inc. Ⓒ PaineWebber
2A Ⓓ Chermayeff & Geismar Inc. Ⓒ National Symphony Orchestra   2B Ⓓ Wages Design Ⓒ Shaw Industries
3A Ⓓ Artimana Ⓒ Moncloa   3B Ⓓ Chase Design Group Ⓒ Gilda Marx

1A **D** Addis **C** iScribe 1B **D** MB Design **C** Scentsations

2A **D** Essex Two Incorporated **C** CIVITAS 2B **D** Chase Design Group **C** The WB

3A **D** Monigle Associates Inc. **C** Crown Vantage 3B **D** Chase Design Group **C** Matteo

D = Design Firm **C** = Client

A

B

Ⓓ = Design Firm   Ⓒ = Client

1A Ⓓ Art Chantry Ⓒ Sub Pop   1B Ⓓ Chermayeff & Geismar Inc. Ⓒ Barneys New York
2A Ⓓ Chase Design Group Ⓒ MSN   2B Ⓓ Design One Ⓒ Colton Groome & Company
3A Ⓓ Kiku Obata & Company Ⓒ Davis Street Land Company   3B Ⓓ Plumbline Studios Ⓒ Six Degrees

1

MARK
LANEGAN
WHISKEY
FOR THE
HOLY
GHOST

BARNEYS
NEW YORK

2

[UNDER
WIRE)

COLTON GROOME
Company

3

PLAZA FRONTENAC

SIX DEGREES

MORGAN STANLEY

RENÉ LEZARD

FOSTER HART
L A W Y E R S

LEUPOLD

COLUMBIA WINERY

M&JWILKOW

A

B

1

2

3

1A ⓓ Chermayeff & Geismar Inc. ⓒ Morgan Stanley 1B ⓓ Simon & Goetz Design ⓒ René Lezard
2A ⓓ Hoyne Design ⓒ Foster Hart Lawyers 2B ⓓ Sandstrom Design ⓒ Leupold
3A ⓓ Phinney/Bischoff Design House ⓒ Columbia Winery - Corus Brands 3B ⓓ Liska + Associates Communication Design ⓒ M&J Wilkow

ⓓ = Design Firm ⓒ = Client

A

B

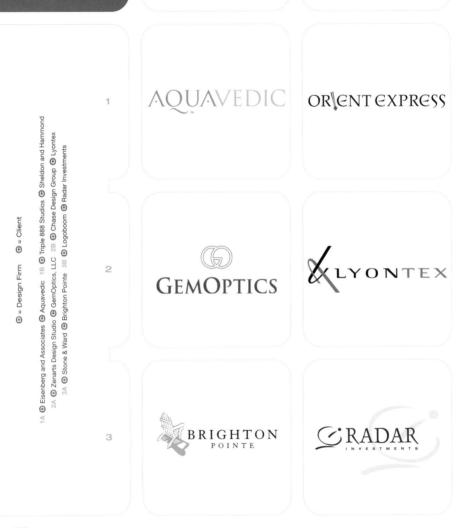

Ⓓ = Design Firm   Ⓒ = Client

1A Ⓓ Eisenberg and Associates Ⓒ Aquavedic 1B Ⓓ Triple 888 Studios Ⓒ Sheldon and Hammond
2A Ⓓ Zenarts Design Studio Ⓒ GemOptics, LLC 2B Ⓓ Chase Design Group Ⓒ Lyontex
3A Ⓓ Stone & Ward Ⓒ Brighton Pointe 3B Ⓓ Logoboom Ⓒ Radar Investments

1

AQUAVEDIC

ORIENT EXPRESS

2

GEMOPTICS

LYONTEX

3

BRIGHTON
POINTE

RADAR
INVESTMENTS

A

B

1

2

3

1A **D** Blue Beetle Design **C** Champs 1B **D** Enterprise IG **C** Monsanto Company

2A **D** Chermayeff & Geismar Inc. **C** World Policy Journal 2B **D** Orange 32 **C** Tastylick Studios

3A **D** Plumbline Studios **C** GarageBand.com 3B **D** Rodgers Townsend **C** Children's Hospital

D = Design Firm **C** = Client

A   B

Ⓓ = Design Firm   Ⓒ = Client

1A Ⓓ Mires Ⓒ Think Outside 1B Ⓓ GTA - Gregory Thomas Associates Ⓒ Litton Industries
2A Ⓓ Chermayeff & Geismar Inc. Ⓒ Mobil Corporation 2B Ⓓ Chermayeff & Geismar Inc. Ⓒ Hansol Paper
3A Ⓓ Chermayeff & Geismar Inc. Ⓒ Feed Magazine 3B Ⓓ Wages Design Ⓒ Assurant Group

A

B

TypeCon2002

Itron

1

Penn

aftermedia.

2

‹ caljisma ›

Chemistry Place

3

1A ⒟ Brian Sooy & Co. ⒞ Society of Typographic Aficionados   1B ⒟ Monigle Associates Inc. ⒞ Itron

2A ⒟ BrandEquity International ⒞ Penn Raquet Sports   2B ⒟ Plumbline Studios ⒞ AfterMedia

3A ⒟ Angryporcupine ⒞ Callisma   3B ⒟ Plumbline Studios ⒞ Addison Wesley Longman

⒟ = Design Firm   ⒞ = Client

A

B

D = Design Firm   C = Client

1A D Braue; Branding & Corporate Design C Gothmann Optik   1B D Chase Design Group C Whodoo
2A D Chermayeff & Geismar Inc. C Ibid Stock Photo   2B D Laura Manthey Design C Blur Convergent Marketing
3A D Kellum McClain Inc. C Bravo Network   3B D Artimana C UOC

	A	B
1	objx	ripe
2	Quris™	KArMA!
3	DAWSON CONSTRUCTION INC	The Museum of Modern Art

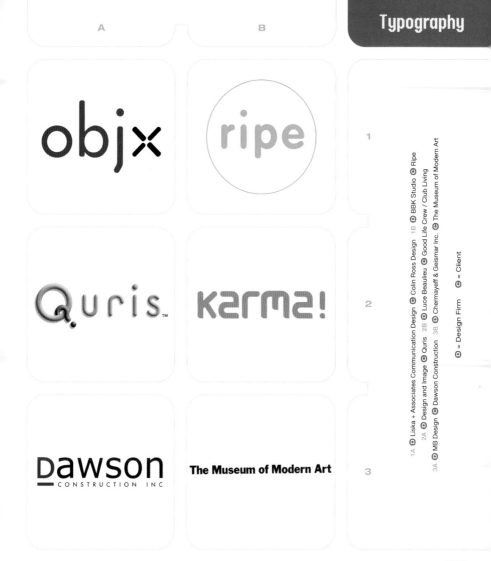

1A Ⓓ Liska + Associates Communication Design Ⓒ Colin Ross Design   1B Ⓓ BBK Studio Ⓒ Ripe

2A Ⓓ Design and Image Ⓒ Quris   2B Ⓓ Luce Beaulieu Ⓒ Good Life Crew / Club Living

3A Ⓓ MB Design Ⓒ Dawson Construction   3B Ⓓ Chermayeff & Geismar Inc. Ⓒ The Museum of Modern Art

Ⓓ = Design Firm   Ⓒ = Client

Typography

A

B

1

2

3

Ⓓ = Design Firm   Ⓒ = Client

1A Ⓓ Start Design Ltd Ⓒ Virgin Atlantic Airways Ltd   1B Ⓓ Start Design Ltd Ⓒ Virgin Atlantic Airways Ltd
2A Ⓓ Addis Ⓒ Helion   2B Ⓓ Chermayeff & Geismar Inc. Ⓒ Precision, Inc.
3A Ⓓ Sandstrom Design Ⓒ adidas International   3B Ⓓ 2b1a Ⓒ Urban Agents

DOVEBID
Business Auctions Worldwide

DiME.

SEKAS

BEST

CUFF

I·N·F·I·N·E·E·R

1

2

3

1A Ⓓ Addis Ⓒ Dovebid 1B Ⓓ Chermayeff & Geismar Inc. Ⓒ Dime Saving Bank of New York

2A Ⓓ Pogon Ⓒ Mapa, Montenegro 2B Ⓓ Chermayeff & Geismar Inc. Ⓒ Best Products

3A Ⓓ Hoyne Design Ⓒ Cuff 3B Ⓓ Chermayeff & Geismar Inc. Ⓒ Infineer

Ⓓ = Design Firm   Ⓒ = Client

	A	B

D = Design Firm   C = Client

1A D Cronan Group C Picnique 1B D Hornall Anderson C Space Needle

2A D Chermayeff & Geismar Inc. C Picnique Frozen Yogurt 2B D Willoughby Design Group C Robyn Nichols

3A D Addis C Aura Cacia 3B D Kiku Obata & Company C The Pageant

A · B

1 · 2 · 3

1A ⓓ Beth Singer Design ⓒ Hillel: The Foundation for Jewish Campus Life 1B ⓓ BrandEquity ⓒ Haworth

2A ⓓ Essex Two Incorporated ⓒ Bell + Howell 2B ⓓ Lexicon Graphix, Inc. ⓒ Jet Black

3A ⓓ Trickett & Webb ⓒ Reuter Brooks Couriers 3B ⓓ Richards Brock Miller Mitchell & Associates ⓒ Cityplace

ⓓ = Design Firm ⓒ = Client

A

B

1

2

3

© = Design Firm   © = Client

1A © Hutchinson Associates, Inc. © Ranger Wireless Solutions   1B © Hornall Anderson © Active Voice
2A © Proart Graphics/Gabriel Kalach © G2 Team Sales   2B © Hornall Anderson © iMind Corporation
3A © Cronan Group © Covia   3B © Hornall Anderson © General Magic

Enclosures

A   B

1

2

3

A

B

1

2

3

1A Ⓓ Addis Ⓒ Exp.com 1B Ⓓ Trickett & Webb Ⓒ Computer Cab PLC
2A Ⓓ Sayles Graphic Design, Inc. Ⓒ Jordan Motors 2B Ⓓ Bright Strategic Design Ⓒ Nutro Products
3A Ⓓ Lieber Cooper Associates Ⓒ Ferrari Ristorante - Chicago, Illinois 3B Ⓓ Ken Shafer Design Ⓒ Sierra On-Line

Ⓓ = Design Firm   Ⓒ = Client

A

B

D = Design Firm　　**C** = Client

1A **D** Brian Sooy & Co. **C** Hypertech Body Building Gear　1B **D** Sackett Design **C** Pacific Foundry
2A **D** Chase Design Group **C** Kemper Snowboards　2B **D** Willoughby Design Group **C** Willoughby Design Group
3A **D** Portal 7 Design **C** Placebo　3B **D** Art Chantry **C** Danger Gens

1

2

3

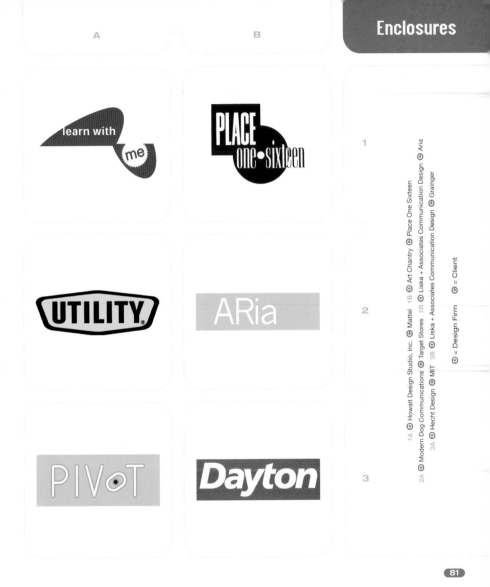

1

2

3

A   B

○ = Design Firm   ● = Client

1A ○ Richards Brock Miller Mitchell & Associates ● Vecta 1B ○ Sandstrom Design ● Tazo Tea
2A ○ Prejean LoBue ● Ristorante Teatro 2B ○ Willoughby Design Group ● Lee Jeans
3A ○ Cato Purnell Partners ● Raffles Hotel 3B ○ Chermayeff & Geismar Inc. ● Eli's Manhattan

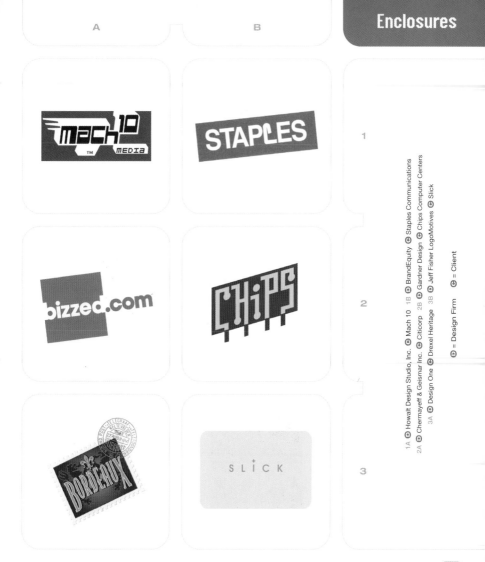

A

B

1

2

3

1A ⒟ Howalt Design Studio, Inc. ⒞ Mach 10   1B ⒟ BrandEquity ⒞ Staples Communications

2A ⒟ Chermayeff & Geismar Inc. ⒞ Citicorp   2B ⒟ Gardner Design ⒞ Chips Computer Centers

3A ⒟ Design One ⒞ Drexel Heritage   3B ⒟ Jeff Fisher LogoMotives ⒞ Slick

ⒹⒹ = Design Firm   ⒞ = Client

⑩ = Design Firm   ⓒ = Client

1A ⑩ Pogon ⓒ Mocca Chocolate Bar 1B ⑩ Liska + Associates Communication Design ⓒ Mr Big Film
2A ⑩ Lieber Cooper Associates ⓒ KIVA - Chicago, Illinois 2B ⑩ Chermayeff & Geismar Inc. ⓒ Pilobolus Dance Company
3A ⑩ Hornall Anderson ⓒ Onkyo Corporation 3B ⑩ Richards Brock Miller Mitchell & Associates ⓒ Know AIDS

1

2

3

A

B

1

2

3

1A **D** Richards Brock Miller Mitchell & Associates **C** Lomas   1B **D** Art Chantry **C** Ompala Square Jungle
2A **D** Chermayeff & Geismar Inc. **C** Liz Claiborne   2B **D** Liska + Associates Communication Design **C** First Aid
3A **D** Art Chantry **C** Free South Africa   3B **D** CRE8 Communications, Inc. **C** Tom Kelby Copywriter

D = Design Firm   **C** = Client

85

A

B

1

2

3

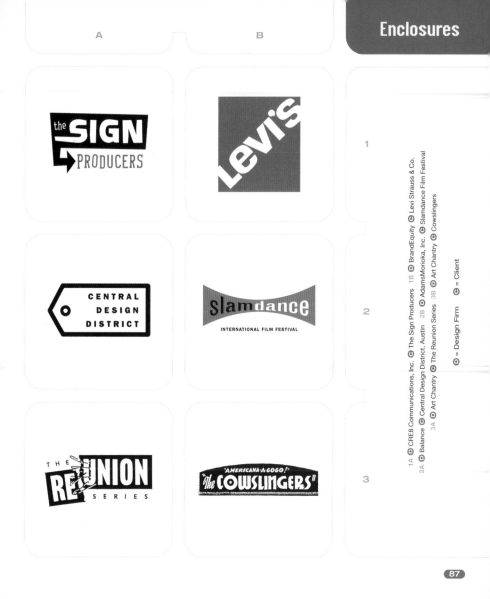

1

2

3

1A **D** CRE8 Communications, Inc. **C** The Sign Producers   1B **D** BrandEquity **C** Levi Strauss & Co.

2A **D** Balance **C** Central Design District, Austin   2B **D** AdamsMorioka, Inc. **C** Slamdance Film Festival

3A **D** Art Chantry **C** The Reunion Series   3B **D** Art Chantry **C** Cowslingers

D = Design Firm   **C** = Client

A

B

1

2

3

D = Design Firm   C = Client

1A D Braue; Branding & Corporate Design C Hans Fiedler Soehne GmbH   1B D Sandstrom Design C Radioland
2A D Mojo Unlimited, LLC C urbanStyle.net   2B D Willoughby Design Group C G. Diebolts
3A D Chase Design Group C Relo Pro, Inc.   3B D Bird Design C In Demand

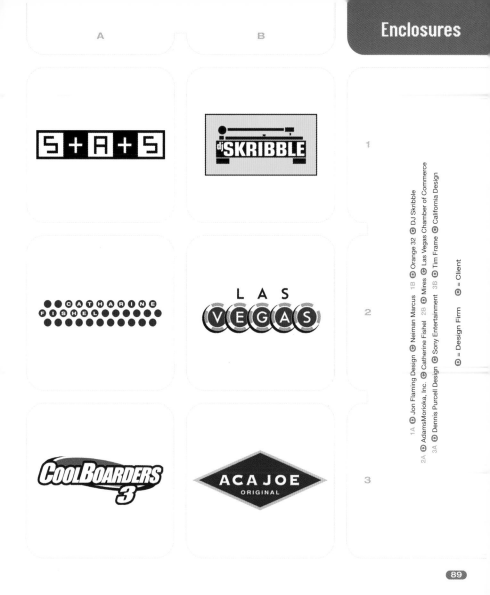

A

B

1

2

3

S + A + S

dj SKRIBBLE

CATHARINE FISHEL

L A S
VEGAS

COOLBOARDERS 3

ACA JOE
ORIGINAL

1A **D** Jon Flaming Design **C** Neiman Marcus   1B **D** Orange 32 **C** DJ Skribble

2A **D** AdamsMorioka, Inc. **C** Catherine Fishel   2B **D** Mires **C** Las Vegas Chamber of Commerce

3A **D** Dennis Purcell Design **C** Sony Entertainment   3B **D** Tim Frame **C** California Design

D = Design Firm   **C** = Client

A   B

Ⓓ = Design Firm   Ⓒ = Client

1A Ⓓ Chase Design Group Ⓒ Kama Sutra   1B Ⓓ Willoughby Design Group Ⓒ Hallmark Flowers
2A Ⓓ Sandstrom Design Ⓒ Levi Strauss & Co.   2B Ⓓ Jon Flaming Design Ⓒ Ken Knight
3A Ⓓ Tim Frame Ⓒ Tim Frame Design   3B Ⓓ AdamsMorioka, Inc. Ⓒ Nickelodeon

1

2

3

A

B

1

2

3

1A Ⓓ Chase Design Group Ⓒ Showtime Networks   1B Ⓓ Howalt Design Studio, Inc. Ⓒ Work, Inc.

2A Ⓓ Device Ⓒ Heart Throbs   2B Ⓓ Sabingrafik Inc. Ⓒ Psytrons

3A Ⓓ Chase Design Group Ⓒ Del the Lagunas Time Tunnel   3B Ⓓ Braue: Branding & Corporate Design Ⓒ Stylus Production

Ⓓ = Design Firm   Ⓒ = Client

A

B

1

2

3

	A	B
1		
2		
3		

1A ⒟ Art Chantry ⒞ Satan's Pilgrims   1B ⒟ Device ⒞ The Horror Special

2A ⒟ Device ⒞ Picture Pocket   2B ⒟ Device ⒞ Power Girl

3A ⒟ Chase Design Group ⒞ Crave Interactive   3B ⒟ Angryporcupine ⒞ Canned Food Alliance

⒟ = Design Firm   ⒞ = Client

A

B

1

2

3

D = Design Firm **C** = Client

1A **D** Willoughby Design Group **C** Rosse Litho 1B **D** Chermayeff & Geismar Inc. **C** Pino Ice Cream and Pastry Shops
2A **D** Howalt Design Studio, Inc. **C** Spinner.com 2B **D** Chase Design Group **C** First Light
3A **D** Planet Propaganda **C** Punch 3B **D** Hoyne Design **C** Zukini

A   B

1   [chickflick]   Tupperware

2   time labs   BLASTER!

3   SCENE OF THE CRIME   artvibe

1A Ⓓ Willoughby Design Group Ⓒ Lee Jeans   1B Ⓓ Chermayeff & Geismar Inc. Ⓒ Tupperware

2A Ⓓ Design Machine Ⓒ Time Labs   2B Ⓓ Art Chantry Ⓒ Blaster

3A Ⓓ Device Ⓒ Scene of the Crime   3B Ⓓ Richard Leland Ⓒ Artvibe.com

Ⓓ = Design Firm   Ⓒ = Client

A

B

1

2

3

A B

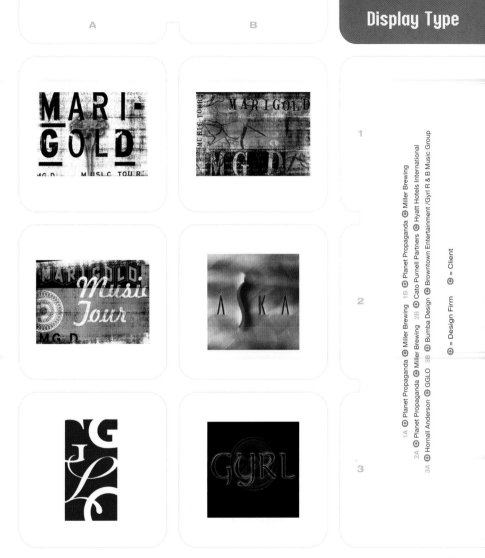

1

2

3

1A **D** Planet Propaganda **C** Miller Brewing 1B **D** Planet Propaganda **C** Miller Brewing

2A **D** Planet Propaganda **C** Miller Brewing 2B **D** Cato Purnell Partners **C** Hyatt Hotels International

3A **D** Hornall Anderson **C** GGLO 3B **D** Bumba Design **C** Browntown Entertainment /Gyrl R & B Music Group

D = Design Firm **C** = Client

Display Type

A

B

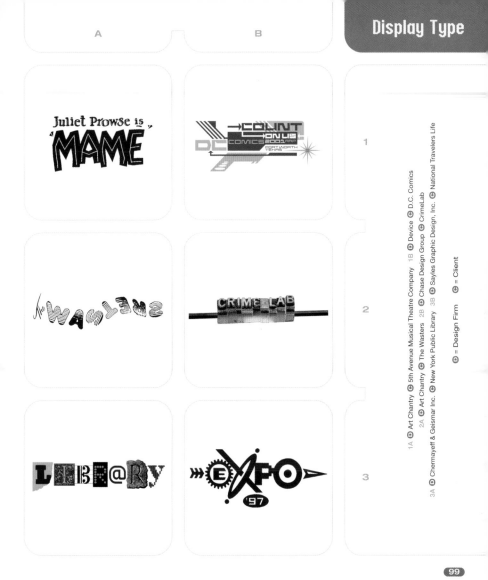

A

B

1

2

3

1A ⓓ Art Chantry ⓒ 5th Avenue Musical Theatre Company 1B ⓓ Device ⓒ D.C. Comics

2A ⓓ Art Chantry ⓒ The Wasters 2B ⓓ Chase Design Group ⓒ CrimeLab

3A ⓓ Chermayeff & Geismar Inc. ⓒ New York Public Library 3B ⓓ Sayles Graphic Design, Inc. ⓒ National Travelers Life

ⓓ = Design Firm   ⓒ = Client

Display Type

Ⓓ = Design Firm   Ⓒ = Client

1A Ⓓ Sandstrom Design Ⓒ Portland Schools Foundation   1B Ⓓ Trickett & Webb Ⓒ Trickett & Webb

2A Ⓓ Hornall Anderson Ⓒ Space Needle   2B Ⓓ Hornall Anderson Ⓒ Say It!

3A Ⓓ Hornall Anderson Ⓒ XOW!   3B Ⓓ James Lienhart Design Ⓒ Yak Central

1

2

1A ⒹKen Shafer Design ⒸOne Reel 1B ⒹKen Shafer Design ⒸSeattle Repertory Theatre

2A ⒹChase Design Group ⒸFax 2B ⒹChase Design Group ⒸThe Alternative Pick

3A ⒹChase Design Group ⒸThe WB 3B ⒹChase Design Group ⒸSemiotext Architecture

Ⓓ = Design Firm Ⓒ = Client

3

Calligraphy

Ⓓ = Design Firm   Ⓒ = Client

1A Ⓓ Be Design Ⓒ Karma Creations   1B Ⓓ Be Design Ⓒ Ohanafarms
2A Ⓓ Chase Design Group Ⓒ MCA Records   2B Ⓓ Chase Design Group Ⓒ Ken Ballard
3A Ⓓ Ken Shafer Design Ⓒ One Reel   3B Ⓓ Chase Design Group Ⓒ Universal Pictures

1

2

3

A	B	
		1
		2
		3

1A **D** Chase Design Group **C** MAD Pictures   1B **D** Chase Design Group **C** Universal Pictures

2A **D** Chase Design Group **C** Chase Design Group   2B **D** Chase Design Group **C** Colossal Pictures

3A **D** Chase Design Group **C** Atlantic Records   3B **D** Chase Design Group **C** Warner Bros. Records

D = Design Firm   **C** = Client

Calligraphy

Ⓓ = Design Firm   Ⓒ = Client

1A Ⓓ Chase Design Group Ⓒ The WB 1B Ⓓ Chase Design Group Ⓒ Apollo Interactive

2A Ⓓ Chase Design Group Ⓒ Virgin Records 2B Ⓓ Chase Design Group Ⓒ Columbia Pictures

3A Ⓓ Chase Design Group Ⓒ Chase Design Group 3B Ⓓ Chase Design Group Ⓒ Maverick Records

1

2

3

A

B

1

2

3

Calligraphy

	A	B

D = Design Firm   **C** = Client

1A **D** Ken Shafer Design **C** Nordstrom   1B **D** Randy Mosher Design **C** MDI, LLC

2A **D** James Lienhart Design **C** Beatrice   2B **D** Ken Shafer Design **C** The Richards Group

3A **D** Chase Design Group **C** Sony Music   3B **D** Chase Design Group **C** Grammercy Pictures

1

2

3

Fred Schneider

johnnies
C A T E R I N G

1

Valentinoise

The
Galaxy Trio

2

Troubled Souls

Muse Air

3

1A Ⓓ Chase Design Group Ⓒ Warner Bros. Records   1B Ⓓ S Design, Inc.   Ⓒ Johnnies Catering

2A Ⓓ Simon & Goetz Design Ⓒ Gmund Buettenpapierfabrik   2B Ⓓ Art Chantry Ⓒ Estrus Records

3A Ⓓ Device Ⓒ Troubled Souls   3B Ⓓ Richards Brock Miller Mitchell & Associates Ⓒ Muse Air

Ⓓ = Design Firm   Ⓒ = Client

A

B

Ⓓ = Design Firm Ⓒ = Client

1A Ⓓ Mitre Design Ⓒ Duhart Creek Winery 1B Ⓓ Minale Tattersfield and Partners Ltd Ⓒ The Refinery

2A Ⓓ Braue; Branding & Corporate Design Ⓒ DuPuis 2B Ⓓ Kontrapunkt Ⓒ Royal Danish Ministry of Foreign Affairs

3A Ⓓ Be Design Ⓒ Hewlett-Packard 3B Ⓓ TBG Design Ⓒ Morris & Raper Realtors

1

Duhart Creek

The Refinery

2

Steven's Brew

Kultūr
MINISTERIET

3

Laser Jet

The Barcelona

1A **Ⓓ** GTA - Gregory Thomas Associates **Ⓒ** Portfolio 1B **Ⓓ** tbg design **Ⓒ** Atlanta Financial Center

2A **Ⓓ** Eisenberg and Associates **Ⓒ** Voltaire Restaurant and Bar 2B **Ⓓ** Cincodemayo **Ⓒ** Malanis [studio]

3A **Ⓓ** CRE8 Communications, Inc. **Ⓒ** NewBait 3B **Ⓓ** Hornall Anderson **Ⓒ** Alta Beverage Company

Ⓓ = Design Firm **Ⓒ** = Client

A

B

D = Design Firm **C** = Client

1A **D** Sibley Peteet Design **C** Gambrinus/Shiner Brewery 1B **D** Design and Image **C** Genki

2A **D** Pat Taylor Inc. **C** Documentary Film Logotype 2B **D** Sayles Graphic Design, Inc. **C** Sun Microsystems

3A **D** Chase Design Group **C** Sony Music 3B **D** Chase Design Group **C** Virgin Records

1

2

3

A

B

1

2

3

1A Ⓓ Braue; Branding & Corporate Design Ⓒ Gollnik Schmiedekunst 1B Ⓓ Chase Design Group Ⓒ Landor & Assoc

2A Ⓓ Ken Shafer Design Ⓒ Her Interactive 2B Ⓓ Chase Design Group Ⓒ Triune Corp.

3A Ⓓ Chase Design Group Ⓒ The WB 3B Ⓓ Chase Design Group Ⓒ Word Records

Ⓓ = Design Firm   Ⓒ = Client

Calligraphy

A

B

D = Design Firm   **C** = Client

1A **D** Hornall Anderson **C** Big Island Candies   1B **D** Randy Mosher Design **C** The Hudson Club Restaurant
2A **D** Randy Mosher Design **C** Spare Time, Inc.   2B **D** Randy Mosher Design **C** Spare Time, Inc.
3A **D** Hornall Anderson **C** Ruby   3B **D** Chase Design Group **C** Chronicle Books

1A Ⓓ Angryporcupine Ⓒ Sharron Kraus   1B Ⓓ Wages Design Ⓒ Kinnett Dairies

2A Ⓓ John Silver Ⓒ Eccleston Square   2B Ⓓ Hornall Anderson Ⓒ Vinifera

3A Ⓓ Artimana Ⓒ Pina   3B Ⓓ Ken Shafer Design Ⓒ One Reel

Ⓓ = Design Firm   Ⓒ = Client

D = Design Firm   **C** = Client

1A **D** Kiku Obata & Company **C** University City & City of St. Louis   1B **D** Chase Design Group **C** Werndorf Associates

2A **D** Sayles Graphic Design, Inc. **C** Gianna Rose   2B **D** Chase Design Group **C** Sega

3A **D** Chase Design Group **C** The Alternative Pick   3B **D** Mires **C** Southern Comfort

A

B

1

2

3

1A ⒹChase Design Group ⒸBuffy the Vampire Slayer 1B ⒹSandstrom Design ⒸESPN
2A ⒹSayles Graphic Design, Inc. ⒸIowa State Fair 2B ⒹSayles Graphic Design, Inc. ⒸHotel Fort Des Moines
3A ⒹGardner Design ⒸExcel Corporation 3B ⒹTim Frame ⒸPressure Connections

Ⓓ = Design Firm   Ⓒ = Client

Crests

A

B

1

2

3

1A Ⓓ Planet Propaganda Ⓒ Eldorado Grill 1B Ⓓ Sayles Graphic Design, Inc. Ⓒ Gianna Rose

2A Ⓓ Chase Design Group Ⓒ Warner Bros. Records 2B Ⓓ Chase Design Group Ⓒ The Alternative Pick

3A Ⓓ Sayles Graphic Design, Inc. Ⓒ Des Moines Plumbing 3B Ⓓ Chase Design Group Ⓒ Capitol Records

A **B**

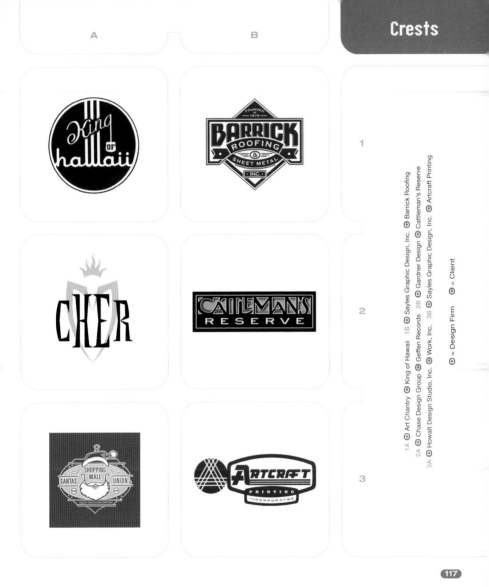

1A **D** Art Chantry **C** King of Hawaii 1B **D** Sayles Graphic Design, Inc. **C** Barrick Roofing

2A **D** Chase Design Group **C** Geffen Records 2B **D** Gardner Design **C** Cattleman's Reserve

3A **D** Howalt Design Studio, Inc. **C** Work, Inc. 3B **D** Sayles Graphic Design, Inc. **C** Artcraft Printing

D = Design Firm **C** = Client

Crests

A

B

1

2

3

A   **B**

1

2

3

1A Ⓓ Willoughby Design Group Ⓒ Willoughby Design Group   1B Ⓓ Howalt Design Studio, Inc. Ⓒ Work, Inc.

2A Ⓓ Hornall Anderson Ⓒ U.S. Cigar   2B Ⓓ Gardner Design Ⓒ Jay Bailey

3A Ⓓ Willoughby Design Group Ⓒ O'Brien Pharmacy   3B Ⓓ Gardner Design Ⓒ Gavin Peters

Ⓓ = Design Firm   Ⓒ = Client

Ⓓ = Design Firm   Ⓒ = Client

1A Ⓓ Jeff Fisher LogoMotives Ⓒ W.C. Winks Hardware   1B Ⓓ Sabingrafik, Inc. Ⓒ Turner Entertainment
2A Ⓓ Sayles Graphic Design, Inc. Ⓒ 3JD   2B Ⓓ Howalt Design Studio, Inc. Ⓒ Work, Inc.
3A Ⓓ Howalt Design Studio, Inc. Ⓒ Main St. Beer   3B Ⓓ Gardner Design Ⓒ River City Brewery

1

2

3

A

B

1

2

3

1A ⓓ Evenson Design Group ⓒ New England Patriots 1B ⓓ Howalt Design Studio, Inc. ⓒ NFL

2A ⓓ Howalt Design Studio, Inc. ⓒ NFL 2B ⓓ Ken Shafer Design ⓒ NFL

3A ⓓ CRE8 Communications, Inc. ⓒ NFL Alumni 3B ⓓ Sandstrom Design ⓒ ESPN

ⓓ = Design Firm   ⓒ = Client

1

2

3

A

B

1

2

3

A

B

1

SWINGLAB™

2

3

Ⓓ = Design Firm   Ⓒ = Client

1A Ⓓ Addis Ⓒ Swinglab 1B Ⓓ CRE8 Communications, Inc. Ⓒ NFL Alumni

2A Ⓓ Sibley Peteet Design Ⓒ Mother Hen Software 2B Ⓓ Sabingrafik, Inc. Ⓒ g.ball.com

3A Ⓓ Cato Purnell Partners Ⓒ Golf Resorts International 3B Ⓓ Sabingrafik, Inc. Ⓒ g.ball.com

A

B

1

2

3

1A ⓓ Gardner Design ⓒ City of Derby   1B ⓓ Richards Brock Miller Mitchell & Associates ⓒ ClubCorp

2A ⓓ Richards Brock Miller Mitchell & Associates ⓒ ClubCorp   2B ⓓ Howalt Design Studio, Inc. ⓒ Peak Experience

3A ⓓ Howalt Design Studio, Inc. ⓒ Peak Experience   3B ⓓ Howalt Design Studio, Inc. ⓒ Peak Experience

ⓓ = Design Firm   ⓒ = Client

Sports

1

2

3

= Design Firm Ⓒ = Client

1A Ⓓ Sabingrafik, Inc. Ⓒ Shimano Resort 1B Ⓓ Kiku Obata & Company Ⓒ Denver Major League Baseball Stadium District

2A Ⓓ Kiku Obata & Company Ⓒ City of Louisville, Kentucky 2B Ⓓ Dotzero Design Ⓒ Star Advisors

3A Ⓓ Felixsockwell.com Ⓒ FakeTV Guide 3B Ⓓ Sandstrom Design Ⓒ ESPN

1

2

3

1A ⓓ Mires ⓒ L.A. Gear   1B ⓓ Rickabaugh Graphics ⓒ Showtime Networks

2A ⓓ Mires ⓒ Nike   2B ⓓ Rickabaugh Graphics ⓒ Big East Conference

3A ⓓ Rickabaugh Graphics ⓒ NBA Properties   3B ⓓ Chase Design Group ⓒ NBA

ⓓ = Design Firm   ⓒ = Client

A

B

① = Design Firm   ② = Client

1A ① Rickabaugh Graphics ② Big East Conference 1B ① Ken Shafer Design ② WNBA
2A ① Ken Shafer Design ② NBA 2B ① Rickabaugh Graphics ② Atlas Color Imaging
3A ① Mires ② Voit Sports 3B ① Rickabaugh Graphics ② NBA Properties

1

2

3

A

B

1

2

3

1A Ⓓ Sibley Peteet Design ⒸJoefan.net 1B ⒹMires ⒸNike

2A ⒹMires ⒸNike 2B ⒹVanderbyl Design ⒸThe Court

3A ⒹRodgers Townsend ⒸRodgers Townsend 3B ⒹRodgers Townsend ⒸRodgers Townsend

Ⓓ = Design Firm Ⓒ = Client

D = Design Firm   C = Client

1A D Dennis Purcell Design C Fox Racing   1B D Rodgers Townsend C East 3
2A D Ken Shafer Design C The Richards Group   2B D Plumbline Studios C Callan Fitness
3A D Sayles Graphic Design, Inc. C Target   3B D Elixir Design C Athleta

A   B

1

2

3

1A ⒟ Sabingrafik, Inc. ⒞ KidsArts San Diego   1B ⒟ Visible Ink Design

2A ⒟ Chermayeff & Geismar Inc. ⒞ Public Broadcasting Service   2B ⒟ Sackett Design ⒞ Biff Henderson

3A ⒟ James Lienhart Design ⒞ The Museum of Science and Industry   3B ⒟ Richards Brock Miller Mitchell & Associates ⒞ Dallas Independent School District

⒟ = Design Firm   ⒞ = Client

A

B

1A Ⓓ Simon & Goetz Design Ⓒ BrandCommunication-one   1B Ⓓ Miaso Design Ⓒ Spartan Development Group, Inc.
2A Ⓓ Prejean LoBue Ⓒ Centurion Technologies   2B Ⓓ Richards Brock Miller Mitchell & Associates Ⓒ The MS Foundation
3A Ⓓ Chase Design Group Ⓒ Toth Advertising   3B Ⓓ Chermayeff & Geismar Inc. Ⓒ Indian Head

1

BC·O

Spartan Development Group
INCORPORATED

2

3

A

B

MERC
D E L I V E R Y

ASSOCIATION OF MATERNAL & CHILD HEALTH PROGRAMS

L A M O P

LAMOP

FOREVIEW

1

2

3

1A ⑩ Dotzero Design ⓒ Merc Delivery   1B ⑩ Beth Singer Design ⓒ Association of Maternal & Child Health Programs

2A ⑩ Planet Propaganda ⓒ LaMop   2B ⑩ Grapefruit Design ⓒ Foreview LLC

3A ⑩ Felixsockwell.com ⓒ Skin Cueticals   3B ⑩ Dogstar ⓒ Cigar Aficionado

⑩ = Design Firm   ⓒ = Client

133

A

B

1

2

3

think

DIGITAL SAVANT

WORK

CLAMPITT PAPER

PAPER PEOPLE

The Ditka Corporation

A   B

1

2

WIGS FOR KIDS

3

AMERICAN HEART ASSOCIATION

ALL KIDS AT HEART

PEP BOYS

MANNY MOE & JACK

1A ⓓ Felixsockwell.com ⓒ Hidden   1B ⓓ Felixsockwell.com ⓒ Creo

2A ⓓ feluxe ⓒ Salons in the Park   2B ⓓ Brian Sooy & Co. ⓒ Wigs for Kids

3A ⓓ Sayles Graphic Design, Inc. ⓒ American Heart Association   3B ⓓ BrandEquity ⓒ The Pep Boys

ⓓ = Design Firm   ⓒ = Client

A

B

1

2

3

A

B

1

2

Frenchbread
PRODUCTIONS

3

MR SWAP.COM

1A Ⓓ Made on Earth Ⓒ Made on Earth   1B Ⓓ Gardner Design Ⓒ Print King

2A Ⓓ Howalt Design Studio, Inc. Ⓒ Calvary Church   2B Ⓓ Dotzero Design Ⓒ Frenchbread Productions

3A Ⓓ Sayles Graphic Design, Inc. Ⓒ A Cut Ahead Hair Salon   3B Ⓓ Be Design Ⓒ Mr.Swap.com

Ⓓ = Design Firm   Ⓒ = Client

A

B

1

2

3

Ⓓ = Design Firm   Ⓒ = Client

1A Ⓓ Sayles Graphic Design, Inc. Ⓒ Sayles Graphic Design, Inc.   1B Ⓓ Sayles Graphic Design, Inc. Ⓒ Phil Goode

2A Ⓓ Braue; Branding & Corporate Design Ⓒ Candy Station   2B Ⓓ Howalt Design Studio, Inc. Ⓒ Work Inc.

3A Ⓓ Angryporcupine Ⓒ Trevor Davies   3B Ⓓ Howalt Design Studio, Inc. Ⓒ Work, Inc. - Design

	A	B
1		

1A Ⓒ CRE8 Communications, Inc. Ⓒ Children's Broadcasting Corp. 1B Ⓓ Sayles Graphic Design, Inc. Ⓒ Annie Meacham

2A Ⓓ Chase Design Group Ⓒ Chase Design Group 2B Ⓓ Mires Ⓒ Cranford Street

3A Ⓓ Art Chantry Ⓒ Scary Stories 3B Ⓓ Planet Propaganda Ⓒ Fringe Hair Studio

Ⓓ = Design Firm   Ⓒ = Client

FRINGE HAIR STUDIO

Heads

A　　　　　B

D = Design Firm　**C** = Client

1A **D** James Lienhart Design **C** Continental Bank Money Card　1B **D** Art Chantry **C** Mike Stein

2A **D** Mires **C** Industry Pictures　2B **D** Lieber Cooper Associates **C** Nebraska Smokehouse Company, Lincoln, Nebraska

3A **D** Sabingrafik, Inc. **C** Nike　3B **D** Gardner Design **C** Reversions Cosmetics

A

B

1

2

3

1A Ⓓ Liska + Associates Communication Design Ⓒ Ohio Made Films   1B Ⓓ Mitre Design Ⓒ Sam Froelich

2A Ⓓ Howalt Design Studio, Inc. Ⓒ Splendid Seed   2B Ⓓ Made on Earth Ⓒ Made on Earth

3A Ⓓ Made on Earth Ⓒ Made on Earth   3B Ⓓ Made on Earth Ⓒ Made on Earth

Ⓓ = Design Firm   Ⓒ = Client

Heads

A

B

1

2

3

A

B

1

2

3

1A ⒟ Essex Two Incorporated ⒞ Indiana Convention and Tourism Bureau   1B ⒟ Pat Taylor Inc. ⒞ National Association for Child Development & Education

2A ⒟ Evenson Design Group ⒞ Izyx   2B ⒟ Modern Dog Communications ⒞ WebTelecom

3A ⒟ Modern Dog Communications ⒞ Nordstrom   3B ⒟ Kellum McClain Inc. ⒞ Topix

⒟ = Design Firm   ⒞ = Client

1

2

3

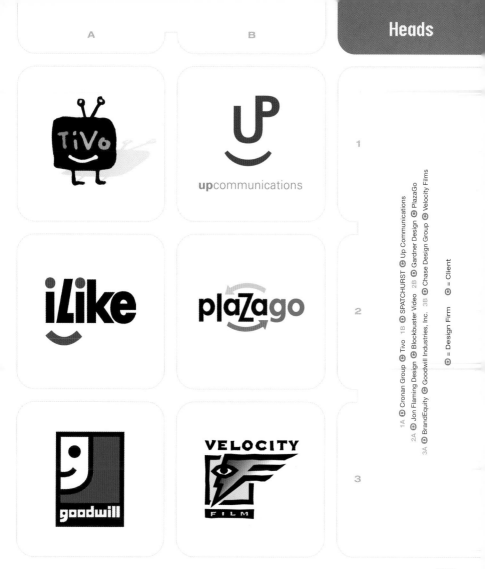

A

B

1

2

3

upcommunications

pla**Za**go

VELOCITY
FILM

1A ⒟ Cronan Group ⒞ Tivo 1B ⒟ SPATCHURST ⒞ Up Communications

2A ⒟ Jon Flaming Design ⒞ Blockbuster Video 2B ⒟ Gardner Design ⒞ PlazaGo

3A ⒟ BrandEquity ⒞ Goodwill Industries, Inc. 3B ⒟ Chase Design Group ⒞ Velocity Films

⒟ = Design Firm   ⒞ = Client

Heads

A B

ⓓ = Design Firm ⓒ = Client

1A ⓓ Miriello Grafico, Inc. ⓒ Newport Coast Oral Facial Institute 1B ⓓ Wages Design ⓒ Relevant Knowledge Research
2A ⓓ Mires ⓒ Copeland Reis 2B ⓓ Art Chantry ⓒ LBJFKKK
3A ⓓ Pat Taylor Inc. ⓒ Ohio Optical 3B ⓓ Howalt Design Studio, Inc. ⓒ X-Ray Vision.net

1

2

3

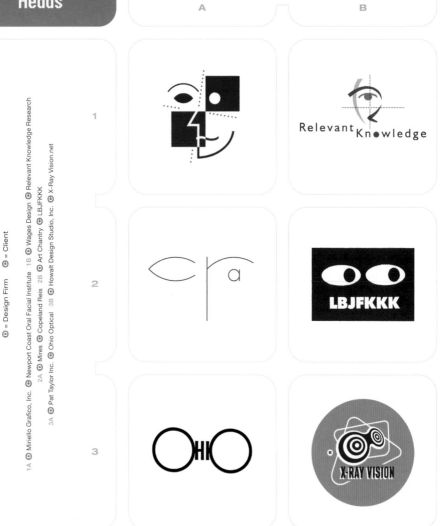

A

B

1

2

3

1A ⓓ Hornall Anderson ⓒ Seattle Convention & Visitors Bureau 1B ⓓ Wages Design ⓒ iTest Assessment

2A ⓓ Dotzero Design ⓒ Kalberer 2B ⓓ Gardner Design ⓒ Virtual Focus

3A ⓓ Pat Taylor Inc. ⓒ Quash Optical 3B ⓓ Sandstrom Design ⓒ Morrow Snowboards

ⓓ = Design Firm   ⓒ = Client

A

B

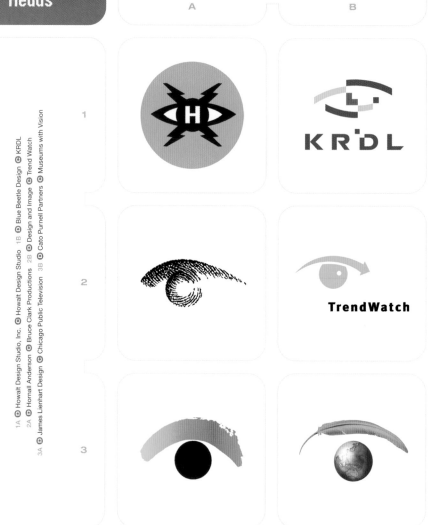

Ⓓ = Design Firm   Ⓒ = Client

1A Ⓓ Howalt Design Studio, Inc. Ⓒ Howalt Design Studio   1B Ⓓ Blue Beetle Design Ⓒ KRDL
2A Ⓓ Hornall Anderson Ⓒ Bruce Clark Productions   2B Ⓓ Design and Image Ⓒ Trend Watch
3A Ⓓ James Lienhart Design Ⓒ Chicago Public Television   3B Ⓓ Cato Purnell Partners Ⓒ Museums with Vision

KRDL

TrendWatch

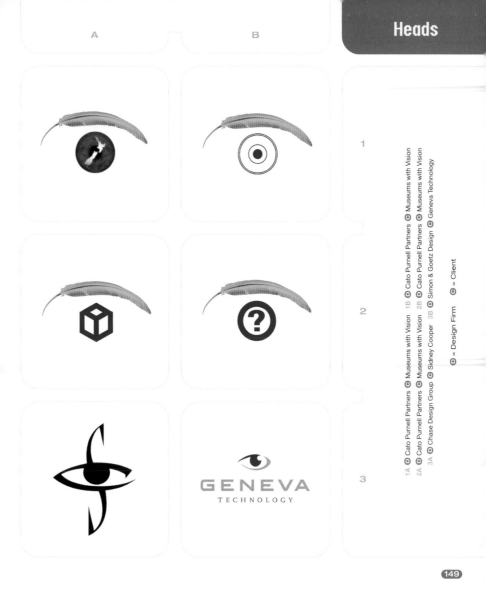

A

B

1

2

3

1A ⒟ Cato Purnell Partners ⒞ Museums with Vision   1B ⒟ Cato Purnell Partners ⒞ Museums with Vision
2A ⒟ Cato Purnell Partners ⒞ Museums with Vision   2B ⒟ Cato Purnell Partners ⒞ Museums with Vision
3A ⒟ Chase Design Group ⒞ Sidney Cooper   3B ⒟ Simon & Goetz Design ⒞ Geneva Technology

⒟ = Design Firm   ⒞ = Client

D = Design Firm   **C** = Client

1A **D** Associated Advertising Agency Inc. **C** Screamingly Different Productions   1B **D** Chernayeff & Geismar Inc. **C** Conversation Trust

2A **D** Chernayeff & Geismar Inc. **C** Time Warner   2B **D** Ken Shafer Design **C** Fox River Paper

3A **D** Mitre Design/Henderson Bromstead Art Co. **C** Digital ESP   3B **D** Artimana **C** Switch

1

2

3

1

2

3

1A **D** Made on Earth **C** Ellen Knable   1B **D** Sibley Peteet Design **C** Charles James

2A **D** Webster Design Associates Inc.   **C** Die Works   2B **D** Webster Design Associates Inc.   **C** Gateway

3A **D** Jon Flaming Design **C** Neiman Marcus   3B **D** Marcus Lee Design **C** Scienceworks Museum

D = Design Firm   **C** = Client

A

B

1

2

3

A

B

1

2

3

Wellsteads

Your healthy alternative to fast food.

SIDEWAYS.com

RADIO VISION

1A ⓓ Marcus Lee Design ⓒ Michael Bone Photography 1B ⓓ Howalt Design Studio, Inc. ⓒ Wellsteads

2A ⓓ Gardner Design ⓒ Kansas State University 2B ⓓ Made on Earth ⓒ Sideways.Com

3A ⓓ Chase Design Group ⓒ Radio Vision 3B ⓓ Jon Flaming Design ⓒ Rand McNally

ⓓ = Design Firm   ⓒ = Client

1

2

3

ⓓ = Design Firm   ⓒ = Client

1A ⓓ Chase Design Group ⓒ Dave Thomas 1B ⓓ Jon Flaming Design ⓒ Objex, Inc.
2A ⓓ Howalt Design Studio, Inc. ⓒ Work, Inc. 2B ⓓ Chase Design Group ⓒ Calypso Films
3A ⓓ Jon Flaming Design ⓒ Skateboarder 3B ⓓ MB Design ⓒ Pacific Marine Foundation

A

B

1

2

3

THE B●WLERS

The Color People

SELECT
Health Products

1A ⒟ Jon Flaming Design ⒞ Mirella Films 1B ⒟ Jon Flaming Design ⒞ Le Gourmand

2A ⒟ Jon Flaming Design ⒞ Bowling Team 2B ⒟ Bright Strategic Design ⒞ Shipper.com

3A ⒟ Design and Image ⒞ The Color People 3B ⒟ Triple 888 Studios ⒞ Select Health

⒟ = Design Firm   ⒞ = Client

A

B

1

2

3

1A ⓓ Henderson Bromstead Art Co. ⓒ Little Theater 1B ⓓ Chermayeff & Geismar Inc. ⓒ Active Aging Association

2A ⓓ feluxe ⓒ eisenberg, TIG 2B ⓓ Mitre Design ⓒ Ashe County

3A ⓓ Bright Strategic Design ⓒ WokStop 3B ⓓ Chermayeff & Geismar Inc. ⓒ Alvin Ailey Dance

ⓓ = Design Firm   ⓒ = Client

A

B

Ⓓ = Design Firm   Ⓒ = Client

1A Ⓓ Gardner Design Ⓒ KJRI 1B Ⓓ Gardner Design Ⓒ Topman
2A Ⓓ Phinney/Bischoff Design House Ⓒ Public Health of King County 2B Ⓓ Indicia Design Inc Ⓒ Digital Crowd, Inc.
3A Ⓓ Bird Design Ⓒ iWin.com 3B Ⓓ Gardner Design Ⓒ Breadar Waggoner Architecture

1

Kansas Joint Replacement Institute

2

Public Health
Seattle & King County
HEALTHY PEOPLE. HEALTHY COMMUNITIES.

DIGITALCROWD

3

iwin·com

A

B

1

2

3

1A ⒟ Howalt Design Studio, Inc. ⒞ Yodlee.com 1B ⒟ Evenson Design Group ⒞ eMaiMai.com

2A ⒟ McMillian Design ⒞ Langton Cherubino 2B ⒟ Felixsockwell.com ⒞ None

3A ⒟ 2b1a ⒞ Bundesverband der Unfallversicherer 3B ⒟ Gardner Design ⒞ Digital Brand Communications

⒟ = Design Firm ⒞ = Client

People

	A	B

A

B

1

2

3

CIBOLA

HASTINGS
FILTERS

PLAY

1A ⒹGardner Design ⒸCibola Restaurant 1B ⒹHenderson Bromstead Art Co. ⒸWake Forest University School of Business

2A ⒹGardner Design ⒸHastings Filters 2B ⒹMires ⒸNeill Archer Roan

3A ⒹGardner Design ⒸThe ArtisTree 3B ⒹHowalt Design Studio, Inc. ⒸWork, Inc.

Ⓓ = Design Firm   Ⓒ = Client

A   B

1   2   3

Ⓓ = Design Firm   Ⓒ = Client

1A Ⓓ Sibley Peteet Design Ⓒ Sicola Martin/Handtech.com 1B Ⓓ Sibley Peteet Design Ⓒ Romano's Macaroni Grill
2A Ⓓ Design and Image Ⓒ Barmon 2B Ⓓ Sayles Graphic Design, Inc. Ⓒ Berlin Packaging
3A Ⓓ Felixsockwell.com Ⓒ Baylor 3B Ⓓ Gardner Design Ⓒ Bravadas Wig Design

A

B

1

2

3

1A ⓓ Enterprise IG ⓒ Monadnock Paper Mills   1B ⓓ Sabingrafik, Inc. ⓒ greens.com

2A ⓓ Addis ⓒ Vectis   2B ⓓ Prejean LoBue ⓒ Lutheran Charity 5k

3A ⓓ Vanderbyl Design ⓒ Digital Engraving   3B ⓓ Vanderbyl Design ⓒ Bedford Properties

ⓓ = Design Firm   ⓒ = Client

A

B

1

2

3

1A Ⓓ Vanderbyl Design Ⓒ Rob Murray   1B Ⓓ Vanderbyl Design Ⓒ Bedford Properties

2A Ⓓ Sanna Design Group, Inc. Ⓒ Allocca, Fardella & Sanna   2B Ⓓ Made on Earth Ⓒ Made on Earth

3A Ⓓ Mitre Design Ⓒ Hutchison Allgood Printing   3B Ⓓ Howalt Design Studio, Inc. Ⓒ Paul Howalt

Ⓓ = Design Firm   Ⓒ = Client

People

D = Design Firm   **C** = Client

1A **D** Simon & Goetz Design **C** Sat1   1B **D** Evenson Design Group **C** Brooks and Howard
2A **D** 2b1a **C** Coffein Delivery   2B **D** Simon & Goetz Design **C** Tony Kappezs
3A **D** Spot Color Incorporated **C** South Riding Proprietary   3B **D** Rickabaugh Graphics **C** Deliverymen

A

B

1

2

3

People

Ⓓ = Design Firm   Ⓒ = Client

1A Ⓓ Jon Flaming Design Ⓒ Sony 1B Ⓓ Rickabaugh Graphics Ⓒ Royal Graphics
2A Ⓓ Grapefruit Design Ⓒ Planigent LLC 2B Ⓓ Howalt Design Studio, Inc. Ⓒ Virgin Records
3A Ⓓ Howalt Design Studio, Inc. Ⓒ Howalt Design 3B Ⓓ Howalt Design Studio, Inc. Ⓒ Fairfax Co, VA

A   B

1

2

3

A

B

1

2

3

1A ⒹHowalt Design Studio, Inc. ⒸBenedictine H.S. 1B ⒹDogstar ⒸRoaring Tiger Films
2A ⒹHowalt Design Studio, Inc. ⒸAustin Skiers 2B ⒹHowalt Design Studio, Inc. ⒸWork, Inc.
3A ⒹMiriello Grafico, Inc. ⒸSan Diego Crew Classic 3B ⒹHoyne Design ⒸTheLounge.com.au

Ⓓ = Design Firm   Ⓒ = Client

169

People

A

B

1

2

3

Ⓓ＝Design Firm　Ⓒ＝Client

1A Ⓓ Prejean LoBue Ⓒ Old El Paso　1B Ⓓ Howalt Design Studio, Inc. Ⓒ Washington Elementary School

2A Ⓓ Howalt Design Studio, Inc. Ⓒ PledgeAllegiance.net　2B Ⓓ Jon Flaming Design Ⓒ Picture This!

3A Ⓓ Howalt Design Studio, Inc. Ⓒ Scout　3B Ⓓ Sayles Graphic Design, Inc. Ⓒ USA Network

A   B

1

2

3

1A ⒟ Howalt Design Studio, Inc. ⒞ Levi Strauss & Co.   1B ⒟ Sabingrafik, Inc. ⒞ Schiedermayer and Associates
2A ⒟ Mitre Design/Henderson Bromstead Art Co. ⒞ Hanes Printables   2B ⒟ Jeff Fisher LogoMotives ⒞ DataDork.com
3A ⒟ Willoughby Design Group ⒞ Bagel & Bagel   3B ⒟ Sabingrafik, Inc. ⒞ Seedworker

⒟ = Design Firm   ⒞ = Client

171

People

A   B

ⓓ = Design Firm   **ⓒ** = Client

1A ⓓ Simon & Goetz Design ⓒ Sachs   1B ⓓ Hornall Anderson ⓒ Yves Veggie Cuisine
2A ⓓ Liska + Associates Communication Design ⓒ Optimistic Camera Company   2B ⓓ Dogstar ⓒ Artisan Films
3A ⓓ Howalt Design Studio, Inc. ⓒ Levi Strauss & Co.   3B ⓓ Cato Purnell Partners ⓒ Grand Hyatt Jakarta

1

2

3

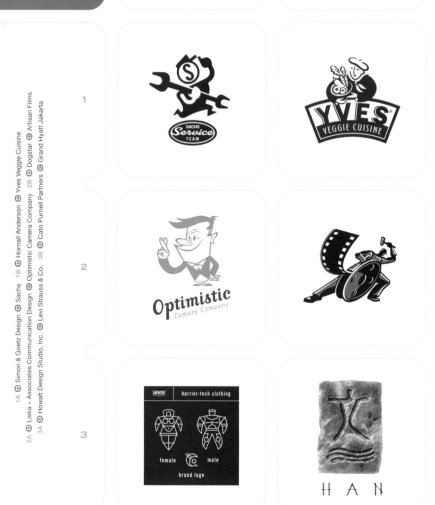

A

B

1

2

3

1A ⒟ Be Design ⒞ Cost Plus World Market   1B ⒟ Sayles Graphic Design, Inc. ⒞ Iowa Metal Fabrication
2A ⒟ Sabingrafik, Inc. ⒞ San Diego Municipal Water District   2B ⒟ Jon Flaming Design ⒞ Living Earth Technology
3A ⒟ Sabingrafik, Inc. ⒞ Almond Board of California   3B ⒟ James Lienhart Design ⒞ Dana

⒟ = Design Firm   ⒞ = Client

A

B

1

2

3

D = Design Firm   **C** = Client

1A **D** Mires **C** Park Blvd. Artworks 1B **D** Dan Stiles Design **C** KALX radio
2A **D** Sabingrafik, Inc. **C** Ear To Ear 2B **D** Sabingrafik, Inc. **C** Sabingrafik, Inc.
3A **D** Webster Design Associates Inc. **C** NE Harvest Beef 3B **D** Mires **C** Green Field Paper Company

1

2

3

1A Ⓓ James Lienhart Design Ⓒ Wild Oats Productions 1B Ⓓ Art Chantry Ⓒ The Mono Men
2A Ⓓ Cincodemayo Ⓒ Cincodemayo 2B Ⓓ Braue; Branding & Corporate Design Ⓒ Joerg Seidel
3A Ⓓ Renegade Design Ⓒ High and Dry Productions 3B Ⓓ Prejean LoBue Ⓒ Ray Hosse - Team Big Head Mountain Bike Group

Ⓓ = Design Firm   Ⓒ = Client

Ⓓ = Design Firm   Ⓒ = Client

1A Ⓓ Device Ⓒ Automatic 1B Ⓓ Visible Ink Design Ⓒ Casino Promotions
2A Ⓓ Chase Design Group Ⓒ Hard Rock Hotel and Casino 2B Ⓓ James Lienhart Design Ⓒ The Art Factory
3A Ⓓ Sabingrafik, Inc. Ⓒ Houghton-Mifflin 3B Ⓓ Chase Design Group Ⓒ Cognito Films

1

2

3

A

B

1

2

3

1A Ⓓ Chase Design Group Ⓒ Tommy Stoilkovich   1B Ⓓ Cato Purnell Partners Ⓒ Grand Hyatt Johor Bahru

2A Ⓓ Device Ⓒ Freak Boarders   2B Ⓓ Henderson Bromstead Art Co. Ⓒ Winston-Salem Foundation

3A Ⓓ MetaDesign Ⓒ Kids Online America   3B Ⓓ Felixsockwell.com Ⓒ O&M

Ⓓ = Design Firm   Ⓒ = Client

A

B

Ⓓ = Design Firm Ⓒ = Client

1A Ⓓ Hoyne Design Ⓒ World Vision Forty Hour Famine 1B Ⓓ Device Ⓒ 100 Bullets
2A Ⓓ Device Ⓒ Resurrection Man 2B Ⓓ Jon Flaming Design Ⓒ Arizona Jeans
3A Ⓓ Jon Flaming Design Ⓒ Cattle Baron's Ball 3B Ⓓ Jon Flaming Design Ⓒ Camp Mak-A-Dream

1

2

3

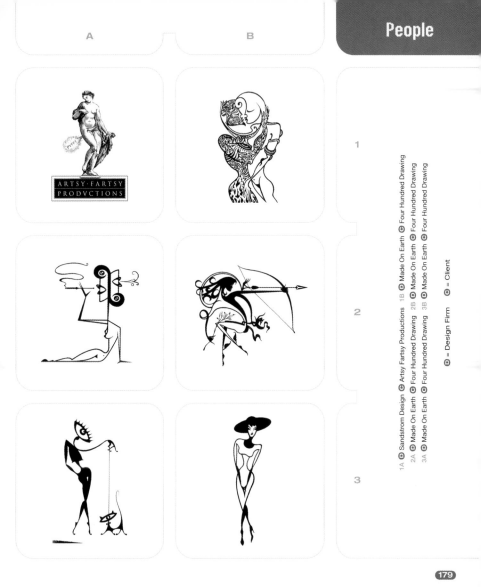

A

B

1

2

3

1A ⒟ Sandstrom Design ⒞ Artsy Fartsy Productions 1B ⒟ Made On Earth ⒞ Four Hundred Drawing
2A ⒟ Made On Earth ⒞ Four Hundred Drawing 2B ⒟ Made On Earth ⒞ Four Hundred Drawing
3A ⒟ Made On Earth ⒞ Four Hundred Drawing 3B ⒟ Made On Earth ⒞ Four Hundred Drawing

⒟ = Design Firm ⒞ = Client

Ⓓ = Design Firm   Ⓒ = Client

1A Ⓓ Made On Earth Ⓒ Four Hundred Hundred Drawing 1B Ⓓ Felixsockwell.com Ⓒ Starwood 3
2A Ⓓ Felixsockwell.com Ⓒ Bob 2B Ⓓ Howalt Design Studio, Inc. Ⓒ Richmond Ballet
3A Ⓓ Felixsockwell.com Ⓒ TV Guide 3B Ⓓ Howalt Design Studio, Inc. Ⓒ Wellstaeds

A

B

1

2

3

1A **D** Studio Rayolux **C** DrunkinSeattle.com 1B **D** Felixsockwell.com **C** Felix Sockwell

2A **D** Henderson Bromstead Art Co. **C** Hanes 2B **D** Wages Design **C** SurfIT.com

3A **D** Wages Design **C** Prevail 3B **D** Jon Flaming Design **C** Elizabeth.Tailor

D = Design Firm **C** = Client

People

Ⓓ = Design Firm   Ⓒ = Client

1A Ⓓ Brian Sooy & Co. Ⓒ Cleveland Clinic   1B Ⓓ Felixsockwell.com Ⓒ Pop Sci
2A Ⓓ Felixsockwell.com Ⓒ None   2B Ⓓ Felixsockwell.com Ⓒ Fake Pearl Head
3A Ⓓ SPATCHURST Ⓒ National Museum of Australia   3B Ⓓ Wages Design Ⓒ American Craft Council's Craft Fair Atlanta

	A	B
1		
2		
3		

A

B

1

2

3

1A Ⓓ Pogon Ⓒ Trend Sport System 1B Ⓓ Cato Purnell Partners Ⓒ Sydney Breast Cancer Institute
2A Ⓓ Gardner Design Ⓒ Glory 2B Ⓓ Felixsockwell.com Ⓒ None
3A Ⓓ Felixsockwell.com Ⓒ None 3B Ⓓ Felixsockwell.com Ⓒ None

Ⓓ = Design Firm Ⓒ = Client

A

B

1

2

3

Ⓓ = Design Firm   Ⓒ = Client

1A Ⓓ Felixsockwell.com Ⓒ None   1B Ⓓ Felixsockwell.com Ⓒ None

2A Ⓓ Felixsockwell.com Ⓒ None   2B Ⓓ Mires Ⓒ Agassi Enterprises

3A Ⓓ Braue; Branding & Corporate Design Ⓒ Optima Wirtschaftsfoerderungskuratorium   3B Ⓓ James Lienhart Design Ⓒ Governors Commission

A

B

VIZIWORX

PASADENA POLICE FOUNDATION

1

2

3

1A ⓓ Gardner Design ⓒ ViziWorx Enhanced Television 1B ⓓ GTA - Gregory Thomas Associates ⓒ Pasadena Police Foundation

2A ⓓ Richards Brock Miller Mitchell & Associates ⓒ Victim's Outreach 2B ⓓ Jon Flaming Design ⓒ Thomas Handy

3A ⓓ Henderson Bromstead Art Co. ⓒ Wake Forest University School of Business 3B ⓓ Felixsockwell.com ⓒ Hand Eye

ⓓ = Design Firm   ⓒ = Client

D = Design Firm   **C** = Client

1A **D** Gardner Design **C** InterFace Computer Consulting   1B **D** Evenson Design Group **C** Heart of Los Angeles Youth
2A **D** Grapefruit Design **C** Le Care Gift Baskets   2B **D** Pat Taylor Inc. **C** Beckie Berez
3A **D** Howalt Design Studio, Inc. **C** Urban Outfitters   3B **D** Gardner Design **C** Envision (services for the blind)

1

2

3

Le Care
Gift baskets

A

B

1

2

3

1A **D** Felixsockwell.com **C** NCAYV, USA   1B **D** Gardner Design **C** The Independent School

2A **D** Hornall Anderson **C** Downtown Seattle Association   2B **D** Howalt Design Studio, Inc. **C** Palm

3A **D** Prejean LoBue **C** Motorola   3B **D** Prejean LoBue **C** Motorola

D = Design Firm   **C** = Client

A B

1

2

3

1A Ⓓ Dotzero Design Ⓒ Star Advisors   1B Ⓓ Sabingrafik, Inc. Ⓒ Voit Sports
2A Ⓓ Plumbline Studios Ⓒ Bigstep   2B Ⓓ Mires Ⓒ Jabra Corporation
3A Ⓓ Dotzero Design Ⓒ Do It For Peace   3B Ⓓ Dotzero Design Ⓒ Do It For Peace

A

B

1

2

3

HANDMADE
in
AMERICA

U.S. DEPARTMENT OF THE INTERIOR

1A ⒟ Dan Stiles Design ⒞ Adventure Music   1B ⒟ Design One ⒞ Handmade in America
2A ⒟ Chase Design Group ⒞ Warner Bros. Records   2B ⒟ Chermayeff & Geismar Inc.   ⒞ United States Department of Interior
3A ⒟ Brian Sooy & Co.   ⒞ Amber Sooy, LMT   3B ⒟ Gardner Design ⒞ Wichita Promise

⒟ = Design Firm   ⒞ = Client

A

B

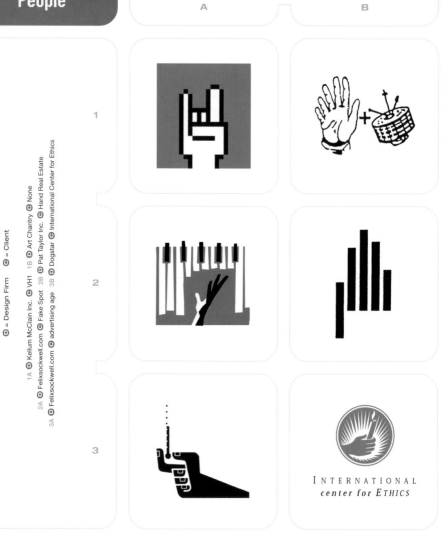

Ⓓ = Design Firm   Ⓒ = Client

1A Ⓓ Kellum McClain Inc. Ⓒ VH1   1B Ⓓ Art Chantry Ⓒ None

2A Ⓓ Felixsockwell.com Ⓒ Fake Spot   2B Ⓓ Pat Taylor Inc. Ⓒ Hand Real Estate

3A Ⓓ Felixsockwell.com Ⓒ advertising age   3B Ⓓ Dogstar Ⓒ International Center for Ethics

INTERNATIONAL
center for ETHICS

A

B

1

2

3

1A Ⓓ Sabingrafik, Inc. Ⓒ AIRS 1B Ⓓ Sabingrafik, Inc. Ⓒ Found Stuff Paperworks
2A Ⓓ Gardner Design Ⓒ Powerhouse 2B Ⓓ Associated Advertising Agency, Inc. Ⓒ Wichita Anesthesiology Chartered
3A Ⓓ Sandstrom Design Ⓒ Clean Water Oregon 3B Ⓓ Felixsockwell.com Ⓒ JWT, Johnson & Johnson

Ⓓ = Design Firm   Ⓒ = Client

Mythology

A   B

A

B

1

2

3

1A Ⓓ Mires Ⓒ Hell Racer 1B Ⓓ Made on Earth Ⓒ Necessary Evil

2A Ⓓ Chase Design Group Ⓒ Yonex 2B Ⓓ Howalt Design Studio, Inc. Ⓒ Diablo Engineering

3A Ⓓ Gardner Design Ⓒ Shift Photography 3B Ⓓ Mires Ⓒ Hell Racer

Ⓓ = Design Firm   Ⓒ = Client

A

B

1

2

3

Ⓓ = Design Firm   Ⓒ = Client

1A Ⓓ Gardner Design Ⓒ Roosevelt Halloween Compact 1B Ⓓ Jon Flaming Design Ⓒ Party Pirates

2A Ⓓ Tim Frame Ⓒ Retro Outfitters 2B Ⓓ Sabingrafik, Inc. Ⓒ Chingones

3A Ⓓ Chase Design Group Ⓒ Nike 3B Ⓓ Art Chantry Ⓒ The Makers

1

2

3

1A ⒟ Howalt Design Studio, Inc. ⒞ Line Red Productions 1B ⒟ Made on Earth ⒞ Made on Earth

2A ⒟ Rickabaugh Graphics ⒞ Players Theatre 2B ⒟ Mires ⒞ Full Bore

3A ⒟ Gardner Design ⒞ Go Away Garage 3B ⒟ Chase Design Group ⒞ Virgin Records

⒟ = Design Firm   ⒞ = Client

Mythology

Ⓓ = Design Firm   Ⓒ = Client

1A Ⓓ Howalt Design Studio, Inc. Ⓒ Splendid Seed   1B Ⓓ Chase Design Group Ⓒ Rod Bone
2A Ⓓ Simon & Goetz Design Ⓒ Reemtsma   2B Ⓓ Made on Earth Ⓒ Made on Earth
3A Ⓓ Art Chantry Ⓒ Estrus Records   3B Ⓓ Chase Design Group Ⓒ Atlantic Records

1

2

3

A

B

1

2

3

1A **D** SPATCHURST **C** City Recital Hall, Angel Place   1B **D** Made on Earth **C** 400 Drawings

2A **D** Tim Frame **C** GSW   2B **D** Treehouse Design **C** Ascension Entertainment

3A **D** Evenson Design Group **C** Angel City Fitness   3B **D** Bumba Design **C** Angel Shack Coffee House

D = Design Firm   **C** = Client

ANGEL CITY
FITNESS

1

THE ANGEL NETWORK

2

GRETZKY
WINGS

3

TRUCKBAY

A

B

1

2

3

1A ⒹBalance ⒸExpress It 1B ⒹChase Design Group ⒸCapitol Records

2A ⒹTreehouse Design ⒸAscension Entertainment 2B ⒹWages Design ⒸAthlete's Foot

3A ⒹGTA - Gregory Thomas Associates ⒸLA Athletic Club 3B ⒹDevice ⒸD.C. Comics

Ⓓ = Design Firm   Ⓒ = Client

THE LOS ANGELES
ATHLETIC CLUB

A

B

1

2

3

ⒹⓂ = Design Firm   ⒸⓂ = Client

1A ⒹMⓂ Device ⒸMⓂ D.C. Comics   1B ⒹMⓂ Howalt Design Studio, Inc.   ⒸMⓂ Warner Bros. (proposed)
2A ⒹMⓂ Device ⒸMⓂ D.C. Comics   2B ⒹMⓂ Chase Design Group   ⒸMⓂ The WB
3A ⒹMⓂ Prejean LoBue ⒸMⓂ Hyatt International - Grand Hyatt Bangkok   3B ⒹMⓂ Gardner Design   ⒸMⓂ Reno Technology

A

B

VIKINGESKIBS
MUSEET

GEBRÜDER SCHAFFRATH
DIAMANTENMANUFAKTUR

1

2

3

1A **D** Kontrapunkt **C** Danish Viking Ship Museum 1B **D** Richards Brock Miller Mitchell & Associates **C** Amerifest

2A **D** Gardner Design **C** Lily Langtry Coach Company 2B **D** Chermayeff & Geismar Inc. **C** Griphon

3A **D** Simon & Goetz Design **C** Gebrüder Schaffrath 3B **D** Sabingrafik, Inc. **C** Turner Entertainment

D = Design Firm   **C** = Client

Mythology

	A	B

A

B

1

2

3

1A Ⓓ Ken Shafer Design Ⓒ Fox River Paper   1B Ⓓ Sabingrafik, Inc. Ⓒ University of California San Diego

2A Ⓓ Prejean LoBue Ⓒ Disneyland Paris - Disney   2B Ⓓ Sabingrafik, Inc. Ⓒ Harcourt & Co.

3A Ⓓ Richards Brock Miller Mitchell & Associates Ⓒ WebGenie   3B Ⓓ Sabingrafik, Inc. Ⓒ Harcourt Brace & Co.

Ⓓ = Design Firm   Ⓒ = Client

Mythology

A

B

1

2

3

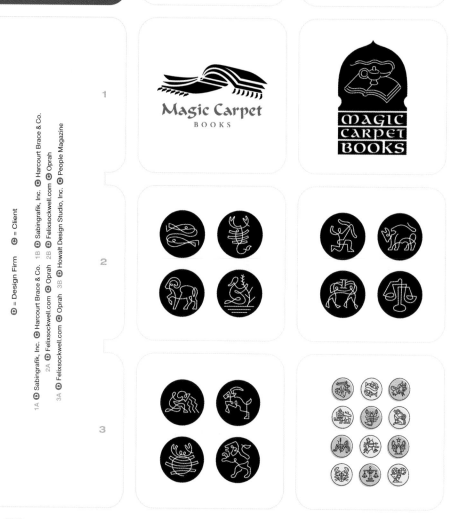

A

B

1

2

3

A

B

1

2

3

A

B

Eagle Ready Mix

1

ALLMERICA
FINANCIAL

2

RED HAWK
INDUSTRIES

RED MOUNTAIN PARK

3

1A Ⓓ Pat Taylor Inc. Ⓒ American Press Agency   1B Ⓓ Hutchinson Associates, Inc. Ⓒ Eagle Ready Mix

2A Ⓓ BrandEquity Ⓒ Allmerica Financial   2B Ⓓ Pat Taylor Inc. Ⓒ U.S. International Trade Commission

3A Ⓓ Design and Image Ⓒ Red Hawk Industries   3B Ⓓ Dogstar Ⓒ Red Mountain Park

Ⓓ = Design Firm   Ⓒ = Client

A

B

1

2

3

Ⓓ = Design Firm   **Ⓒ** = Client

1A Ⓓ BIRD Design Ⓒ BIRD Design   1B Ⓓ Gardner Design Ⓒ Neufeldt's

2A Ⓓ Dogstar Ⓒ Gregory Freeze   2B Ⓓ Mitre Design/Henderson Bromstead Art Co. Ⓒ Habitat For Humanity

3A Ⓓ Balance Ⓒ Ambleside School   3B Ⓓ Sibley Peteet Design Ⓒ Tequila Mockingbird

1

2

3

1A ⓓ Felixsockwell.com ⓒ The Old Crow 1B ⓓ Pogon ⓒ Idea Plus DDB

2A ⓓ Gardner Design ⓒ Fat Chance Bird Food 2B ⓓ Prejean LoBue ⓒ The Kitchen Inc.

3A ⓓ Artomat Design ⓒ Seattle Symphony 3B ⓓ Gardner Design ⓒ John Crowe Photography

ⓓ = Design Firm   ⓒ = Client

① = Design Firm ⑥ = Client

1A ① Chermayeff & Geismar Inc. ⑥ Savories 1B ① Chermayeff & Geismar Inc. ⑥ St. Joe Real Estate
2A ① Klauddesign ⑥ Microsoft 2B ① Lexicon Graphix, Inc. ⑥ Terakeet
3A ① GTA - Gregory Thomas Associates ⑥ Airescue 3B ① CRE8 Communications, Inc. ⑥ Abused Adult Resource Center

1

2

3

A

B

1

2

3

1A ⒟ Associated Advertising Agency Inc. ⒞ Malisa's Hope   1B ⒟ Dotzero Design ⒞ Do It For Peace

2A ⒟ Sabingrafik, Inc. ⒞ Canyon Hills   2B ⒟ Sabingrafik, Inc. ⒞ Canyon Hills

3A ⒟ Sabingrafik, Inc. ⒞ Pardee Homes   3B ⒟ Miriello Grafico, Inc. ⒞ The Irvine Company

⒟ = Design Firm   ⒞ = Client

A   B

Ⓓ = Design Firm   Ⓒ = Client

1A Ⓓ Associated Advertising Agency, Inc. Ⓒ Occidental Management   1B Ⓓ Chase Design Group Ⓒ Hum

2A Ⓓ Monigle Associates Inc. Ⓒ Camden Properties   2B Ⓓ Cincodemayo Ⓒ Direct Link

3A Ⓓ SPATCHURST Ⓒ Capitol Theatre   3B Ⓓ Chermayeff & Geismar Inc. Ⓒ National Broadcasting Company

1

2

3

A

B

1

2

3

1A Ⓓ Chase Design Group Ⓒ Hard Rock Hotel and Casino 1B Ⓓ Dogstar Ⓒ Peacock Music Studio
2A Ⓓ Dotzero Design Ⓒ Wichita Blues Society 2B Ⓓ Modern Dog Communications Ⓒ One Reel
3A Ⓓ Webster Design Associates Inc. Ⓒ Thunderbird Grill 3B Ⓓ Gardner Design Ⓒ Corrington High School

Ⓓ = Design Firm   Ⓒ = Client

213

① = Design Firm ⓒ = Client

1A ① Prejean LoBue ⓒ Red Hot Pepper Sauce 1B ① Sandstrom Design ⓒ Chickenville
2A ① Luce Beaulieu ⓒ restaurant Le Poulet Grillé 2B ① Jon Flaming Design ⓒ Early Bird Records
3A ① Cincodemayo ⓒ Cerro Brujo 3B ① Howalt Design Studio, Inc. ⓒ Hanschell Innis

1

2

3

A

B

1

2

3

CHICKENVILLE

· CAPONS ·
ROTISSERIE CHICKEN

WICHITA
FARM & ART
MARKET

the Owl and the Pussycat
children's outfitters

1A ⒟ Sandstrom Design ⒞ Burgerville 1B ⒟ Hornall Anderson ⒞ Capons Rotisserie Chicken
2A ⒟ Gardner Design ⒞ Wichita Farm and Art Market 2B ⒟ Pat Taylor Inc. ⒞ Night Owl Security
3A ⒟ TBG Design ⒞ The Owl & Pussycat 3B ⒟ Vanderbyl Design ⒞ Bedford Properties

⒟ = Design Firm   ⒞ = Client

A

B

1

2

3

Ⓓ = Design Firm   Ⓒ = Client

1A Ⓓ Tharp Did It Ⓒ Bayshore Press   1B Ⓓ Gardner Design Ⓒ Kansas Health Foundation
2A Ⓓ Sabingrafik, Inc. Ⓒ Bridgewater   2B Ⓓ Chermayeff & Geismar Inc. Ⓒ Desert Ranch
3A Ⓓ Be Design Ⓒ Slave   3B Ⓓ Jeff Fisher LogoMotives Ⓒ Jeff Fisher LogoMotives

Brightwater

SLAVE

A

B

1

2

3

1A Ⓓ Chermayeff & Geismar Inc. Ⓒ Crane and Company 1B Ⓓ Sandstrom Design Ⓒ Blue Heron Ale

2A Ⓓ Chermayeff & Geismar Inc. Ⓒ Key Sabinal 2B Ⓓ Marcus Lee Design Ⓒ Hobsons Bay City Council

3A Ⓓ Evenson Design Group Ⓒ Discovery Island 3B Ⓓ Sabingrafik, Inc. Ⓒ San Diego Zoo

Ⓓ = Design Firm   Ⓒ = Client

A

B

⊕ = Design Firm   ⊖ = Client

1A ⊖ Felixsockwell.com ⊕ Turtle Creek Chorale 1B ⊖ Addis ⊕ Archipelago
2A ⊖ Chermayeff & Geismar Inc. ⊕ Tennessee Aquarium 2B ⊖ Sabingrafik, Inc. ⊕ The Masters Group
3A ⊖ Richards Brock Miller Mitchell & Associates ⊕ Triton 3B ⊖ Sibley Peteet Design ⊕ Center For Marine Conservation

1

ARCHIPELAGO

2

3

TRITON

A

B

1

2

3

1A Ⓓ Marcus Lee Design Ⓒ Frankston City Council   1B Ⓓ Eisenberg and Associates Ⓒ University of Arizona

2A Ⓓ Made on Earth Ⓒ Fat Fish Films   2B Ⓓ Prejean LoBue Ⓒ Atlantis Paradise Island

3A Ⓓ Triple 888 Studios Ⓒ Sundance Seafoods   3B Ⓓ Artimana Ⓒ Mako Software

Ⓓ = Design Firm   Ⓒ = Client

A

B

1

2

3

D = Design Firm   **C** = Client

1A **D** Pogon **C** Konoba Pantagana   1B **D** Sabingrafik, Inc. **C** Tamarindo Pacifico
2A **D** Sabingrafik, Inc. **C** Chaos Lures   2B **D** Dogstar **C** San Roc Cay
3A **D** Jeff Fisher LogoMotives **C** Triangle Productions!   3B **D** Simon & Goetz Design **C** Supmarine

A

B

1

2

3

1A **D** Prejean LoBue **C** Hyatt International - Grand Hyatt Bali   1B **D** Dogstar **C** Cathy Fishel

2A **D** Dogstar **C** Black Warrior Cahaba Rivers Land Trust   2B **D** Mitre Design **C** Pam Fish, production/design

3A **D** Chermayeff & Geismar Inc. **C** National Aquarium Baltimore   3B **D** Tharp Did It **C** Steamer's Grillhouse

D = Design Firm   **C** = Client

A

B

D = Design Firm   **C** = Client

1A **D** Chermayeff & Geismar Inc. **C** New England Aquarium 1B **D** John Evans Design **C** Salt Grass Steakhouse

2A **D** Gardner Design **C** Piranha Manufacturing 2B **D** Bel Bare **C** Kailis Bros

3A **D** Gardner Design **C** Kona Coast 3B **D** Sayles Graphic Design, Inc. **C** Aventis

1

2

piranha

IRONWORKERS • PRESS BRAKES • SHEARS

BLUE FISH

3

kona coast

ST. LUCIA

A   **B**

1

2

3

1A ⓓ Gardner Design ⓒ Great Lodge   1B ⓓ CRE8 Communications, Inc. ⓒ Green River Stone Company

2A ⓓ Chase Design Group ⓒ Heal the Bay   2B ⓓ Gardner Design ⓒ Big Fish Bar

3A ⓓ Gardner Design ⓒ Go Away Garage   3B ⓓ Made on Earth ⓒ Made on Earth

ⓓ = Design Firm   ⓒ = Client

Fish, Bugs, Reptiles

A

B

1

2

3

D = Design Firm   **C** = Client

1A **D** Gardner Design **C** Buzz Cut Lawn Care 1B **D** Gardner Design **C** KTBN Kansas Technology Business Network

2A **D** Simon & Goetz Design **C** Red Ant 2B **D** Klauddesign **C** Make a Wish

3A **D** GTA - Gregory Thomas Associates **C** Monarch Films 3B **D** Sayles Graphic Design, Inc. **C** McArthur Company

1A **D** Woodhead International **C** Betty Blue 1B **D** Mitre Design **C** Good Lawn

2A **D** Simon & Goetz Design **C** Lakepaper 2B **D** Art Chantry **C** Estrus Records

3A **D** Sabingrafik, Inc. **C** Sabingrafik, Inc. 3B **D** Howalt Design Studio, Inc. **C** Webdrop

D = Design Firm   **C** = Client

Ⓓ = Design Firm   Ⓒ = Client

1A Ⓓ Chase Design Group Ⓒ Virgin Records   1B Ⓓ Made on Earth Ⓒ Ariat
2A Ⓓ Gardner Design Ⓒ Go Away Garage   2B Ⓓ Chermayeff & Geismar Inc. Ⓒ Clay Adams
3A Ⓓ Wages Design Ⓒ Atlanta Medical Group   3B Ⓓ Artimana Ⓒ Modo Arquitectura

1

2

3

A   B

1

2

3

1A **D** James Lienhart Design **C** Chameleon Color Crafts   1B **D** Be Design **C** Cost Plus World Market

2A **D** Liska + Associates Communication Design **C** Reptile Artists Agent   2B **D** Webster Design Associates Inc. **C** Croc's Bar & Grill

3A **D** Chase Design Group **C** Ammirati Puris Lintas   3B **D** DK Design **C** Six Flags Over Texas

D = Design Firm   **C** = Client

Animals

A

B

1

2

3

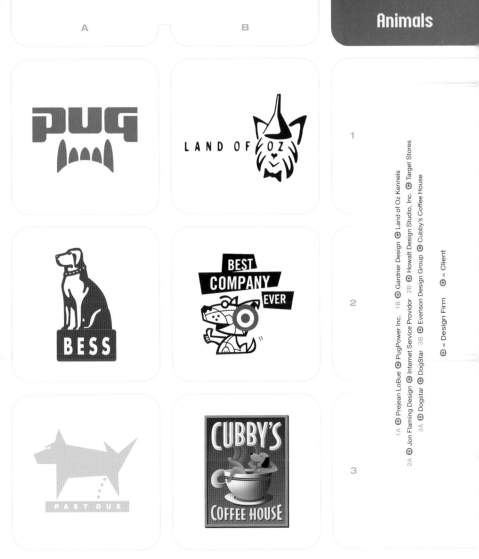

A

B

1

2

3

1A Ⓓ Prejean LoBue Ⓒ PugPower Inc. 1B Ⓓ Gardner Design Ⓒ Land of Oz Kennels
2A Ⓓ Jon Flaming Design Ⓒ Internet Service Providor 2B Ⓓ Howalt Design Studio, Inc. Ⓒ Target Stores
3A Ⓓ Dogstar 3B Ⓓ Evenson Design Group Ⓒ Cubby's Coffee House

Ⓓ = Design Firm   Ⓒ = Client

A

B

1

2

3

= Design Firm   = Client

1A Dogstar DogStar   1B Sandstrom Design Pavlov Productions
2A Made on Earth Made on Earth   2B Dogstar Dogstar
3A Howalt Design Studio, Inc. Levi-Strauss   3B Dogstar Dogstar

A   B

1A **D** Art Chantry **C** Mexican Doorbell 1B **D** Gardner Design **C** Sheldon Coleman

2A **D** Dogstar **C** Dogstar 2B **D** Pat Taylor Inc. **C** Dirty Paws

3A **D** Dogstar **C** DogStar 3B **D** Chase Design Group **C** Madeleine Clark

D = Design Firm   **C** = Client

A

B

Ⓓ = Design Firm   Ⓒ = Client

1A Ⓓ Sibley Peteet Design Ⓒ Scotland Yards Fabric 1B Ⓓ Jon Flaming Design Ⓒ Racehound

2A Ⓓ Zenarts Design Studio Ⓒ Petswelcome.com 2B Ⓓ Rickabaugh Graphics Ⓒ Northern Illinois University

3A Ⓓ Prejean LoBue Ⓒ Cabella 3B Ⓓ Made on Earth Ⓒ Made on Earth

	A	B
1	prairie dog	
2	SUNDOG	
3		

1A **D** Chase Design Group **C** Robert Yang 1B **D** Gardner Design **C** Avalanche Popcorn

2A **D** Planet Propaganda **C** Sundog 2B **D** Richards Brock Mitchell & Associates **C** Lewisville Humane Society

3A **D** Jon Flaming Design **C** Petigree 3B **D** Sanna Design Group, Inc. **C** Animal Krackers Grooming, Inc.

D = Design Firm   **C** = Client

Ⓓ = Design Firm   Ⓒ = Client

1A Ⓓ Evenson Design Group Ⓒ Pet Net 1B Ⓓ Vanderbyl Design Ⓒ Heinz

2A Ⓓ Wages Design Ⓒ DeKalb Humane Society 2B Ⓓ Art Chantry Ⓒ Chuckie-Boy Records

3A Ⓓ Made on Earth Ⓒ Made on Earth 3B Ⓓ Howalt Design Studio, Inc. Ⓒ Roseville Cougars

1

2

3

A

B

1

2

3

1A ⒹAfter Hours Creative ⒸMax and Lucy 1B ⒹMade on Earth ⒸMade on Earth
2A ⒹPhinney/Bischoff Design House ⒸTorrefazione Italia 2B ⒹChase Design Group ⒸLeaping Manx
3A ⒹDogstar ⒸThe Cat 3B ⒹGardner Design ⒸThe Independent School

Ⓓ = Design Firm Ⓒ = Client

235

ⓓ = Design Firm ⓒ = Client

1A ⓓ Sabingrafik, Inc. ⓒ San Diego Zoo 1B ⓓ Gardner Design ⓒ PrairieFest
2A ⓓ Ken Shafer Design ⓒ The Richards Group, Team Mad Dog 2B ⓓ Sabingrafik, Inc. ⓒ San Diego Gas & Electric
3A ⓓ Vanderbyl Design ⓒ Coyote Books 3B ⓓ Simon & Goetz Design ⓒ ADP Engineering GMBH / Rotwild

A

B

1

2

3

BROWN DEER
PRESS

WILDBEASTS
GLOBAL CONSERVATION PROJECT
SAN DIEGO ZOO

DALLAS ZOO

1A Ⓓ Sabingrafik, Inc. Ⓒ Harcourt & Co. 1B Ⓓ Sabingrafik, Inc. Ⓒ San Diego Zoo

2A Ⓓ Richards Brock Miller Mitchell & Associates Ⓒ Oryx 2B Ⓓ Richards Brock Miller Mitchell & Associates Ⓒ The Dallas Zoo

3A Ⓓ Hornall Anderson Ⓒ Gang of Seven 3B Ⓓ Chermayeff & Geismar Inc. Ⓒ Ibex Wear

Ⓓ = Design Firm   Ⓒ = Client

Animals

A   B

D = Design Firm   **C** = Client

1A **D** Essex Two Incorporated **C** Arlington International   1B **D** Rickabaugh Graphics **C** PAVE Advertising

2A **D** Simon & Goetz Design **C** Winning Wheels   2B **D** Sabingrafik, Inc. **C** Freelance Productions

3A **D** Sabingrafik, Inc. **C** McMillin Communities   3B **D** Jeff Fisher LogoMotives **C** Sisters Rodeo Assocation

1

2

3

UNION

RANCHO DOS CAÑADAS

SISTERS RODEO CELEBRATING 60 YEARS

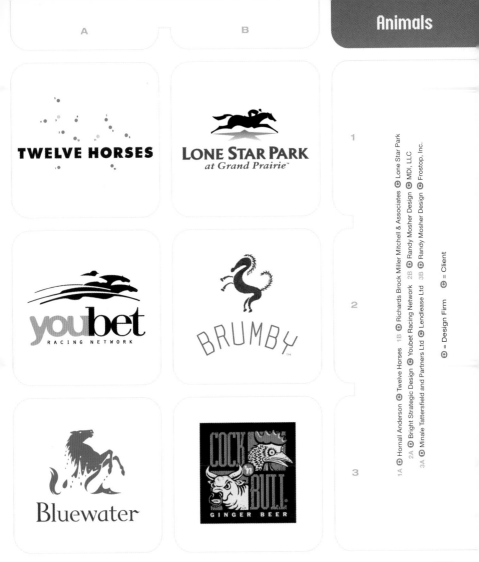

A   B

1   2   3

1A Ⓓ Hornall Anderson Ⓒ Twelve Horses   1B Ⓓ Richards Brock Miller Mitchell & Associates Ⓒ Lone Star Park
2A Ⓓ Bright Strategic Design Ⓒ Youbet Racing Network   2B Ⓓ Randy Mosher Design Ⓒ MDi, LLC
3A Ⓓ Minale Tattersfield and Partners Ltd Ⓒ Lendlease Ltd   3B Ⓓ Randy Mosher Design Ⓒ Frostop, Inc.

Ⓓ = Design Firm   Ⓒ = Client

Animals

	A	B

A

B

1

2

3

CROSSINGS At The Riverhouse

HOCH HAUS 1967 Cotta Park

BURLY BEAR network

1A ⓓ Vanderbyl Design ⓒ Bedford Properties 1B ⓓ Gardner Design ⓒ Doskocil Meats

2A ⓓ Jeff Fisher LogoMotives ⓒ Crossings at The Riverhouse 2B ⓓ Gardner Design ⓒ Hoch Haus Cabin

3A ⓓ Howalt Design Studio, Inc. ⓒ Burly Bear Television 3B ⓓ Prejean LoBue ⓒ Southwest Missouri State University

ⓓ = Design Firm   ⓒ = Client

A

B

Ⓓ = Design Firm   Ⓒ = Client

1A Ⓓ Howalt Design Studio, Inc. Ⓒ Burly Bear TV   1B Ⓓ Balance Ⓒ Koala

2A Ⓓ Sabingrafik, Inc. Ⓒ Big Behr Design Co.   2B Ⓓ Vanderbyl Design Ⓒ California Conservation Corp

3A Ⓓ Richards Brock Miller Mitchell & Associates Ⓒ Bearsouls   3B Ⓓ Willoughby Design Group Ⓒ Peruvian Connection

1

2

3

Hungry Minds™

HIDING
◟P L A C E◞

1A ⒟ Addis ⒞ IDG books 1B ⒟ James Lienhart Design ⒞ Black Sheep Club

2A ⒟ Sibley Peteet Design ⒞ Quiet Time 2B ⒟ Balance ⒞ Hiding Place

3A ⒟ Sayles Graphic Design, Inc. ⒞ Beaverdale Neighborhood Association 3B ⒟ Sayles Graphic Design, Inc. ⒞ Racoon River Brewing Company

⒟ = Design Firm   ⒞ = Client

A

B

1A Ⓓ Made on Earth Ⓒ Made on Earth 1B Ⓓ Prejean LoBue Ⓒ Disney Cruise Line - Disney

2A Ⓓ Richards Brock Miller Mitchell & Associates Ⓒ Young President's Organization 2B Ⓓ Gardner Design Ⓒ Blue Hat Media

3A Ⓓ Be Design Ⓒ digiScents 3B Ⓓ Sabingrafik, Inc. Ⓒ Monkey Studios

1

"squeak"

2

bluehat

M E D I A • • • • •

3

MONKEY STUDIOS

A

B

1A **D** Sabingrafik, Inc. **C** San Diego Zoo   1B **D** Device **C** Blag!

2A **D** Sabingrafik, Inc. **C** Tamarindo Diria   2B **D** Prejean LoBue **C** Chris Gray

3A **D** Chase Design Group **C** Save The Rainforest   3B **D** Sabingrafik, Inc. **C** The Davis Family

D = Design Firm   **C** = Client

Animals

D = Design Firm   C = Client

1A D Sabingrafik, Inc. C San Diego Zoo 1B D Webster Design Associates Inc. C Webster Design
2A D Sandstrom Design C Nissan/TBWA Chiat Day 2B D John Evans Design C Purple Giraffe T-Shirt Co.
3A D Eisenberg and Associates C Tucson Zoological Society 3B D Chase Design Group C Atherton

A

B

1A ⒹKiku Obata & Company ⒸSt. Louis Zoo 1B ⒹSabingrafik, Inc. ⒸHelen Woodward Animal Center

2A ⒹSpiral Design Studio ⒸMapInfo Corporation 2B ⒹGardner Design ⒸKansas Humane Society

3A ⒹAfter Hours Creative ⒸOBCTV 3B ⒹSabingrafik, Inc. ⒸLincoln Park Zoo

Ⓓ = Design Firm Ⓒ = Client

D = Design Firm   **C** = Client

1A **D** Webster Design Associates Inc. **C** Arcosanti Homes   1B **D** Miriello Grafico, Inc. **C** Twin Oaks

2A **D** Dotzero Design **C** Bonneville Environmental Foundation   2B **D** GTA - Gregory Thomas Associates **C** Greentree Pictures

3A **D** Sayles Graphic Design, Inc. **C** Cohabaco Cigar Co   3B **D** Addis **C** Consensus Health

Arcosanti Homes, Inc.

Twin Oaks

GREEN TAGS

greentree
p i c t u r e s

COHABACO
CIGAR CO

consensus
HEALTH

Integrated Choices for Whole Health

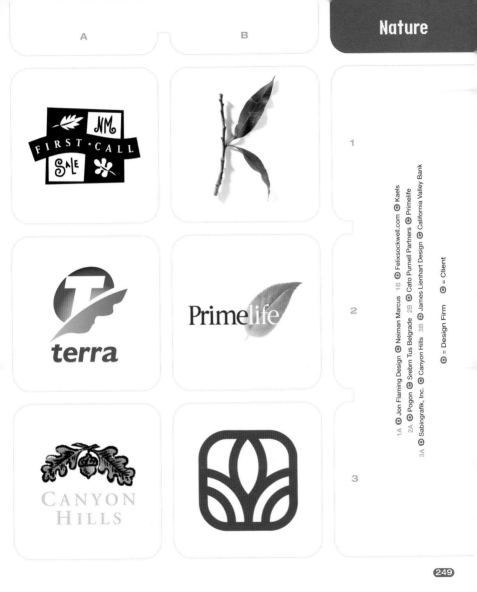

1A Ⓓ Jon Flaming Design Ⓒ Neiman Marcus 1B Ⓓ Felixsockwell.com Ⓒ Kaels

2A Ⓓ Pogon Ⓒ Srebrn Tus Belgrade 2B Ⓓ Cato Purnell Partners Ⓒ Primelife

3A Ⓓ Sabingrafik, Inc. Ⓒ Canyon Hills 3B Ⓓ James Lienhart Design Ⓒ California Valley Bank

Ⓓ = Design Firm   Ⓒ = Client

249

Nature

A   B

1

2

3

D = Design Firm   C = Client

1A D Miriello Grafico, Inc. C Rancho Bernardo Inn   1B D Be Design C Frontier Natural Products

2A D Bright Strategic Design C Tree People   2B D Evenson Design Group C DoubleGreen Landscapes

3A D Elixir Design C New Leaf Paper   3B D Marcus Lee Design C Se'madi

simply
Organic™

DOUBLE GREEN
LANDSCAPES

NEW LEAF
PAPER

se'madi

1

2

3

1A ⓓ Willoughby Design Group ⓒ Hallmark 1B ⓓ Howalt Design Studio, Inc. ⓒ Sears
2A ⓓ Wages Design ⓒ Rivermoore Park 2B ⓓ Treehouse Design ⓒ Treehouse Design
3A ⓓ Sibley Peteet Design ⓒ Ed Windler 3B ⓓ Orange 32 ⓒ Guidance Wholistic Health

ⓓ = Design Firm   ⓒ = Client

A

B

1

KGRO

INOCHI

2

TRANSITION HOUSE

TERRA NOVA
NURSERIES, INC.

3

THE
GARDEN
LOUNGE

D = Design Firm   **C** = Client

1A **D** BrandEquity **C** KMart Corporation 1B **D** Liska + Associates Communication Design **C** Inochi
2A **D** Hecht Design **C** Transition House 2B **D** Jeff Fisher LogoMotives **C** Terra Nova Nurseries
3A **D** Prejean LoBue **C** Hyatt International - Grand Hyatt Bangkok 3B **D** John Evans Design **C** Big Green Plants.com

A

B

1

2

3

1A Ⓓ Design and Image ⒼGrassroots Market 1B ⒹPlumbline Studios ⒼProvencia

2A ⒹJohn Silver ⒼChristian Life School 2B ⒹBlue Beetle Design ⒼRisis

3A ⒹJon Flaming Design ⒼLiving Earth Technology 3B ⒹChermayeff & Geismar Inc. ⒼTulip Films

Ⓓ = Design Firm   Ⓒ = Client

A

B

1

2

3

Caboodles

EXECUTIVE

e
g

effortless gardening

flowerpower

GRANDIFLORUM

PERFUMES

1A ⓓ Mires ⓒ Caboodles   1B ⓓ Willoughby Design Group ⓒ Stuart Hall

2A ⓓ Planet Propaganda ⓒ effortless gardening   2B ⓓ Proart Graphics/Gabriel Kalach ⓒ Flower Power

3A ⓓ Elixir Design ⓒ Grandiflorum Perfumes   3B ⓓ Pat Taylor Inc. ⓒ International Peace Garden Foundation

ⓓ = Design Firm   ⓒ = Client

A

B

D = Design Firm   **C** = Client

1A **D** Chermayeff & Geismar Inc. **C** White House Conference on Children 1B **D** Sayles Graphic Design, Inc. **C** Pattee Enterprises
2A **D** GTA - Gregory Thomas Associates **C** USC 2B **D** Henderson Bromstead Art Co. **C** Somerset Homes
3A **D** Miriello Grafico, Inc. **C** D'Olivo 3B **D** S Design, Inc. **C** Oklahoma Garden Festival Foundation

1

2

3

UNIVERSITY/
EXPOSITION
PARK

SOMERSET
C O U R T

OKLAHOMA
GARDEN
FESTIVAL

A

B

1

2

3

1A ⒟ Pogon ⒞ Podrum Palić   1B ⒟ Hornall Anderson ⒞ Best Cellars

2A ⒟ Prejean LoBue ⒞ The King Ranch Vineyard Partnership   2B ⒟ Sibley Peteet Design ⒞ O's Campus Cafe

3A ⒟ Marcus Lee Design ⒞ Xyzest   3B ⒟ Sibley Peteet Design ⒞ Tim McClure

⒟ = Design Firm   ⒞ = Client

Ⓓ = Design Firm   Ⓒ = Client

1A Ⓓ Hornall Anderson Ⓒ Best Cellars   1B Ⓓ Sackett Design Ⓒ Nightshade Restaurant
2A Ⓓ Marcus Lee Design Ⓒ CherryPrint   2B Ⓓ Sayles Graphic Design, Inc. Ⓒ Bell's Apple Orchard
3A Ⓓ Balance Ⓒ Heartsmart   3B Ⓓ Sayles Graphic Design, Inc. Ⓒ Bell's Apple Orchard

A
B

THE COTTON CENTER

Greenwood Park

Rancho Bernardo Inn

1

2

3

1A **D** Sabingrafik, Inc. **C** Found Stuff Paperworks 1B **D** After Hours Creative **C** The Cotton Center
2A **D** Prejean LoBue **C** Assemblies of God Church 2B **D** Gardner Design **C** Midwest Ag. Board of Trade
3A **D** Modern Dog Communications **C** Greenwood Parks Dept. 3B **D** Sabingrafik, Inc. **C** Rancho Bernardo Inn

D = Design Firm   **C** = Client

1

2

3

Ⓓ = Design Firm   Ⓒ = Client

1A Ⓓ Sibley Peteet Design Ⓒ Bodhi Yoga   1B Ⓓ Dogstar Ⓒ Birmingham Ecoplex

2A Ⓓ CRE8 Communications, Inc. Ⓒ Interior Gardens   2B Ⓓ Pat Taylor Inc. Ⓒ Trees America

3A Ⓓ MB Design Ⓒ Barkley Corporation   3B Ⓓ Miriello Grafico, Inc. Ⓒ Lone Cypress Importers

INTERIOR
GARDENS

TreesAmerica

BARKLEY
D I S T R I C T

Lone Cypress
IMPORTERS

PURVEYORS OF FINE WINES
SAN DIEGO, CA
& WINE MERCHANDISE

A

B

1

2

3

THE CYPRESS CENTER

Verrazzano

EAGLE LAKE ON ORCAS ISLAND

1A ⒟ Prejean LoBue ⒞ The Callaway Bank   1B ⒟ Buz Design Group ⒞ University of Southern California

2A ⒟ Mires ⒞ Shea Homes   2B ⒟ Dogstar ⒞ Woodland Village Retirement Community

3A ⒟ Treehouse Design ⒞ The Cypress Center   3B ⒟ Hornall Anderson ⒞ Eagle Lake on Orcas Island

⒟ = Design Firm   ⒞ = Client

D = Design Firm   **C** = Client

1A **D** Evenson Design Group **C** Eras Center   1B **D** Mires **C** Adventure 16
2A **D** Sayles Graphic Design, Inc. **C** Alpine Shop   2B **D** Simon & Goetz Design **C** ZDF
3A **D** Chermayeff & Geismar Inc. **C** United States Department of the Interior   3B **D** Design and Image **C** Landesign

1

2

3

1A Ⓓ BrandEquity Ⓒ Earth Shoe 1B Ⓓ Chermayeff & Geismar Inc. Ⓒ Turning Stone Casino

2A Ⓓ Hornall Anderson Ⓒ Heavenly Stone 2B Ⓓ Sabingrafik, Inc. Ⓒ Canyon Hills

3A Ⓓ Mires Ⓒ Nextec 3B Ⓓ Cato Purnell Partners Ⓒ Docklands School of Design

Ⓓ = Design Firm   Ⓒ = Client

Ⓓ = Design Firm   Ⓒ = Client

1A Ⓓ Mires Ⓒ The Church of Today 1B Ⓓ Sibley Peteet Design Ⓒ Bares Capital Management
2A Ⓓ Richards Brock Miller Mitchell & Associates Ⓒ WaterDesk.com 2B Ⓓ Brian Sooy & Co. Ⓒ Great Lakes Technology Park
3A Ⓓ Sackett Design Ⓒ Charles Schwab 3B Ⓓ Monigle Associates Inc. Ⓒ Riverside Health

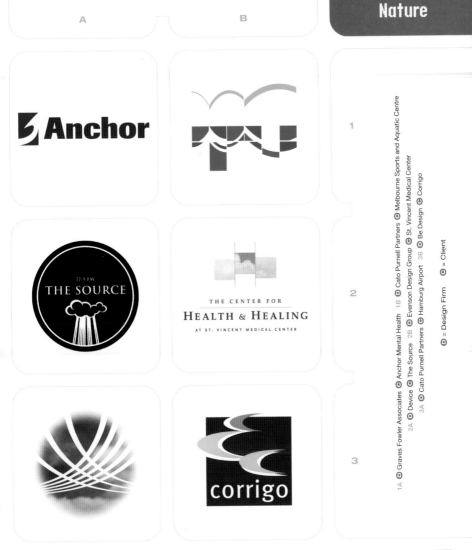

A
B

1

2

3

1A ⒟ Graves Fowler Associates ⒞ Anchor Mental Health   1B ⒟ Cato Purnell Partners ⒞ Melbourne Sports and Aquatic Centre

2A ⒟ Device ⒞ The Source   2B ⒟ Evenson Design Group ⒞ St. Vincent Medical Center

3A ⒟ Cato Purnell Partners ⒞ Hamburg Airport   3B ⒟ Be Design ⒞ Corrigo

⒟ = Design Firm   ⒞ = Client

265

Nature

	A	B
1		 AL DEMNA WATERFRONT PROJECT
2	 DueWest	
3	 **13**	

Ⓓ = Design Firm   Ⓒ = Client

1A Ⓓ James Lienhart Design Ⓒ Spectrum   1B Ⓓ Design and Image Ⓒ Al Demna
2A Ⓓ Design and Image Ⓒ Due West   2B Ⓓ Kellum McClain Inc. Ⓒ The Actors Ensemble
3A Ⓓ Chermayeff & Geismar Inc. Ⓒ Artear Television Network   3B Ⓓ Chermayeff & Geismar Inc. Ⓒ Ring of Fire Aquarium, Osaka, Japan

A

B

1

2

3

SOLARIAN.

Active for Life

1A ⒟ Sabingrafik, Inc. ⒞ Cranford Group   1B ⒟ Dotzero Design ⒞ Jodie Day
2A ⒟ Be Design ⒞ Armstrong   2B ⒟ Sandstrom Design ⒞ Sokol Blosser Winery
3A ⒟ Graves Fowler Associates ⒞ Robert Wood Johnson   3B ⒟ Cato Purnell Partners ⒞ Snow Hydro Electricity

⒟ = Design Firm   ⒞ = Client

A

B

1

2

3

A

B

1

2

3

1A Ⓓ Gardner Design Ⓒ Virtual Focus 1B Ⓓ Sabingrafik, Inc. Ⓒ Taylor Guitars
2A Ⓓ Planet Propaganda Ⓒ Brave World Productions 2B Ⓓ Tim Frame Ⓒ Universal Studios
3A Ⓓ Modern Dog Communications Ⓒ American Design & Manufacturing 3B Ⓓ Roman Design Ⓒ EdGate.com, Inc.

Ⓓ = Design Firm   Ⓒ = Client

Shapes

A | B

D = Design Firm   **G** = Client

1A **D** Jon Flaming Design **G** Global Partners   1B **D** Cronan Group **G** eWorldFreight

2A **D** Chermayeff & Geismar Inc. **G** Pan American Airways   2B **D** Gardner Design **G** La Chance International Brokerage

3A **D** Sabingrafik, Inc. **G** Brightwater   3B **D** Sabingrafik, Inc. **G** Found Stuff Paperworks

A

B

1

2

3

1A ⓒ Chermayeff & Geismar Inc. ⓒ National Credit Bank of Russia 1B ⓓ Gardner Design ⓒ TumbleDrum

2A ⓓ Sabingrafik, Inc. ⓒ Oliver McMillin 2B ⓓ Cincodemayo ⓒ Interexpo

3A ⓓ Be Design ⓒ Be Design 3B ⓓ Eisenberg and Associates ⓒ Blockbuster Productions

ⓓ = Design Firm ⓒ = Client

A

B

1

2

3

D = Design Firm   **C** = Client

1A **D** Cincodemayo **C** Bar Celona   1B **D** Dotzero Design **C** Planet Salon

2A **D** Cincodemayo **C** Frisa   2B **D** Hornall Anderson **C** Bogart Golf

3A **D** Design and Image **C** Brad Adams Walker   3B **D** James Lienhart Design **C** MLR Design

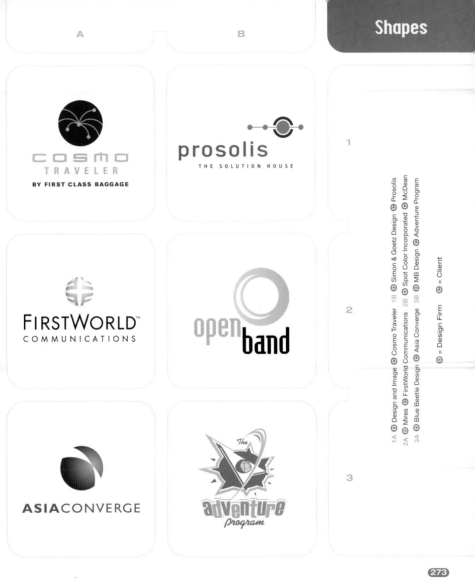

A

B

1

2

3

1A **D** Design and Image **C** Cosmo Traveler 1B **D** Simon & Goetz Design **C** Prosolis

2A **D** Mires **C** FirstWorld Communications 2B **D** Spot Color Incorporated **C** McDean

3A **D** Blue Beetle Design **C** Asia Converge 3B **D** MB Design **C** Adventure Program

D = Design Firm **C** = Client

A

B

1

2

3

Ⓓ = Design Firm   Ⓒ = Client

1A Ⓓ Howalt Design Studio, Inc. Ⓒ Mach 10   1B Ⓓ Design and Image Ⓒ Doom

2A Ⓓ Chermayeff & Geismar Inc. Ⓒ Pan American World Congress of Architects, Washing   2B Ⓓ Cato Purnell Partners Ⓒ The Federal Group

3A Ⓓ Cronan Group Ⓒ Kintana   3B Ⓓ Lieber Cooper Associates Ⓒ Swissotel - Chicago, Illinois

A B

1

2

3

1A **D** John Silver **C** John Silver Design 1B **D** Mires **C** Powertrax

2A **D** Cato Purnell Partners **C** Neil Henson Fashion Bytes 2B **D** Hornall Anderson **C** Aerzone Corporation

3A **D** Wages Design **C** Weather Channel 3B **D** Cronan Group **C** TeaLeaf Technology

D = Design Firm **C** = Client

A

B

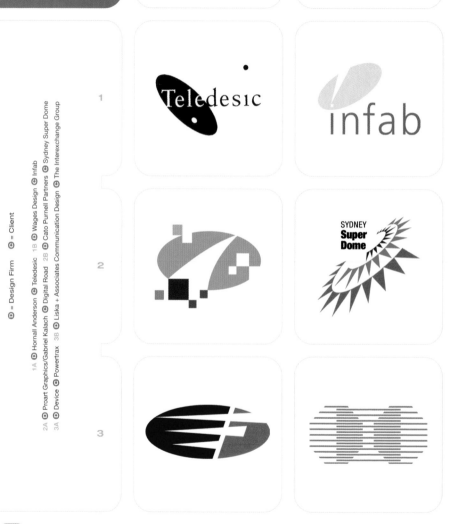

D = Design Firm   **C** = Client

1A **D** Hornall Anderson **C** Teledesic   1B **D** Wages Design **C** Infab
2A **D** Proart Graphics/Gabriel Kalach **C** Digital Road   2B **D** Cato Purnell Partners **C** Sydney Super Dome
3A **D** Device **C** Powertrax   3B **D** Liska + Associates Communication Design **C** The Interexchange Group

1

2

3

A

B

1

2

3

1A Ⓓ Planet Propaganda Ⓒ Stir   1B Ⓓ Indicia Design Inc Ⓒ TriActive, Inc.

2A Ⓓ Mires Ⓒ Invitrogen Life Technologies   2B Ⓓ Plumbline Studios Ⓒ International Sites

3A Ⓓ Corporate Image Consultants, Inc. Ⓒ Sales Mark, Inc.   3B Ⓓ Design and Image Ⓒ Lofts on Park Avenue

Ⓓ = Design Firm   Ⓒ = Client

A

B

1

2

3

A

B

BOSTON MEDIA
CORPORATION

SCKK
Statens Center for
Kompetence- og
Kvalitetsudvikling

INSIGHT
ASSESSMENT

1A ⓓ Grapefruit Design ⓒ Boston Media Corporation 1B ⓓ Kontrapunkt ⓒ Danish National Center for the Development of Competence and Quality
2A ⓓ Plumbline Studios ⓒ Insight Assessment 2B ⓓ Sanna Design Group Inc. ⓒ Comnet Telecom Supply
3A ⓓ Cato Purnell Partners ⓒ Schein Bayer 3B ⓓ Plumbline Studios ⓒ Opux

ⓓ = Design Firm   ⓒ = Client

1

2

3

A

B

1

2

3

D = Design Firm   **C** = Client

1A **D** Lieber Cooper Associates **C** Swissotel - Chicago, Illinois   1B **D** Planet Propaganda **C** Interactive Media Solutions

2A **D** Prejean LoBue **C** Healthcare Solutions Inc.   2B **D** Vanderbyl Design **C** Yachtsmans Exchange

3A **D** Cato Purnell Partners **C** Primrose   3B **D** Mires **C** Fusion Media

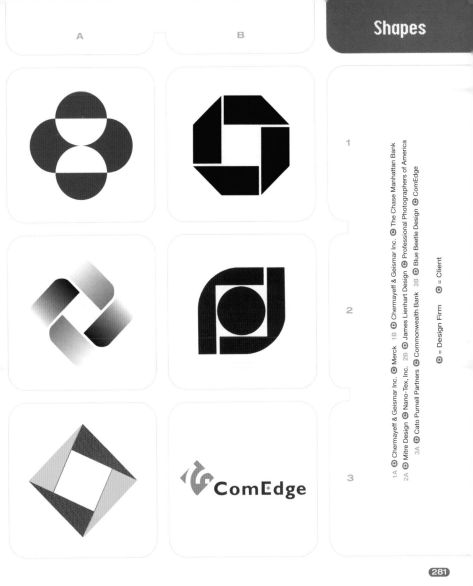

A

B

1

2

3

1A ⒹChermayeff & Geismar Inc. ⒸMerck 1B ⒹChermayeff & Geismar Inc. ⒸThe Chase Manhattan Bank
2A ⒹMitre Design ⒸNano-Tex, Inc. 2B ⒹJames Lienhart Design ⒸProfessional Photographers of America
3A ⒹCato Purnell Partners ⒸCommonwealth Bank 3B ⒹBlue Beetle Design ⒸComEdge

Ⓓ = Design Firm   Ⓒ = Client

ComEdge

Shapes

A   B

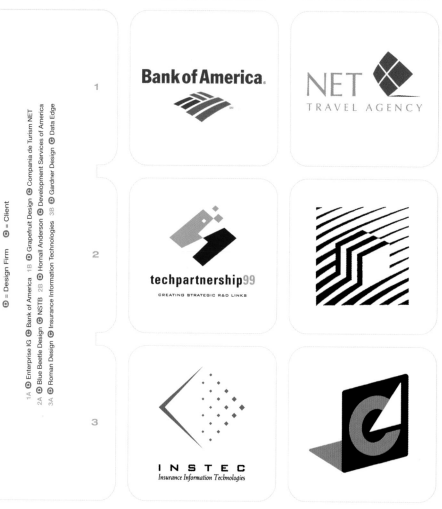

◐ = Design Firm   ◉ = Client

1A ◐ Enterprise IG ◉ Bank of America   1B ◐ Grapefruit Design ◉ Compania de Turism NET
2A ◐ Blue Beetle Design ◉ NSTB   2B ◐ Hornall Anderson ◉ Development Services of America
3A ◐ Roman Design ◉ Insurance Information Technologies   3B ◐ Gardner Design ◉ Data Edge

Bank of America.

NET
TRAVEL AGENCY

techpartnership99

CREATING STRATEGIC R&D LINKS

I N S T E C
Insurance Information Technologies

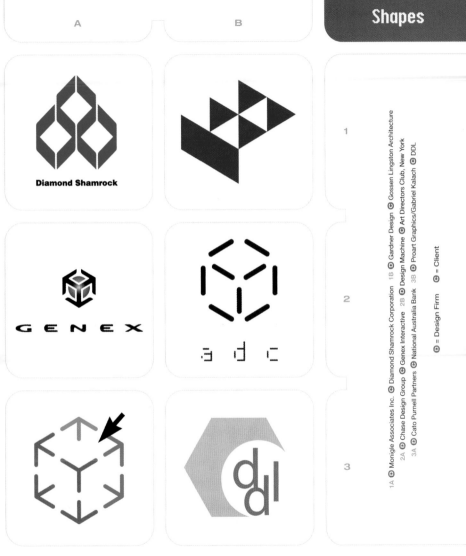

A

B

1

2

3

Diamond Shamrock

GENEX

1A ⒹMongle Associates Inc. ⒸDiamond Shamrock Corporation 1B ⒹGardner Design ⒸGossen Lingston Architecture
2A ⒹChase Design Group ⒸGenex Interactive 2B ⒹDesign Machine ⒸArt Directors Club, New York
3A ⒹCato Purnell Partners ⒸNational Australia Bank 3B ⒸProart Graphics/Gabriel Kalach ⒸDDL

Ⓓ = Design Firm   Ⓒ = Client

○ = Design Firm ○ = Client

1A ○ Be Design ○ Be Design ○ Mitre Design ○ Studio Place Photography
2A ○ Gardner Design ○ Thermos Nissan 2B ○ Chase Design Group ○ Robert Yang
3A ○ Sackett Design ○ Cliffside Entertainment 3B ○ SPATCHURST ○ Australian Water and Coastal Studies

1

2

3

A

B

WORLDSONG
2002 MUSICAL SUPERCONNECTIVITY

VelociGen Inc.

1

glide

TalkOn

2

TECHNOLOGY
ACHIEVEMENT
AWARD 2000

tradelets.com

3

1A **D** Chase Design Group **C** Santa Fe Creatives 1B **D** Miriello Grafico, Inc. **C** VelociGen Inc.

2A **D** Brian Sooy & Co. **C** Great Lakes Incubator for Developing Enterprises 2B **D** Klauddesign **C** Microsoft

3A **D** Blue Beetle Design **C** NSTB 3B **D** Grapefruit Design **C** Netprise, Inc.

D = Design Firm   **C** = Client

Shapes

A

B

1

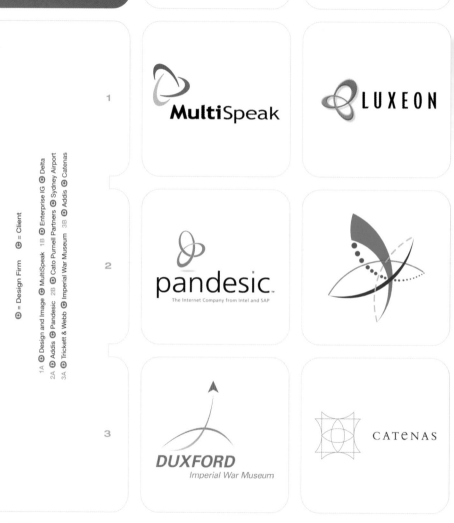

MultiSpeak

LUXEON

2

pandesic.
The Internet Company from Intel and SAP

3

DUXFORD
Imperial War Museum

CATENAS

A

B

EMBARCADERO COMMON

billerbeck
SCHLAFKULTUR SEIT 1921

sunesis

LOYANG POINT

okamoto

energex

1

2

3

1A Ⓓ Klauddesign Ⓒ Embarcadero Common 1B Ⓓ Simon & Goetz Design Ⓒ Billerbeck Betten
2A Ⓓ Chase Design Group Ⓒ Sunesis 2B Ⓓ Blue Beetle Design Ⓒ HDB
3A Ⓓ Hornall Anderson Ⓒ Okamoto Corporation 3B Ⓓ Cato Purnell Partners Ⓒ Energex Australia

Ⓓ = Design Firm   Ⓒ = Client

Symbols

A   B

1

2

3

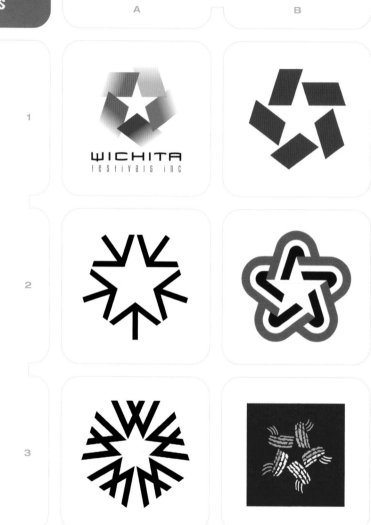

A

B

1

2

3

PENTACASAS

STRATEGIC
AIR & SPACE
MUSEUM

1A ⓓ Braue; Branding & Corporate Design ⓒ Pentacasas Ferienhaeuser GmbH   1B ⓓ Sibley Peteet Design ⓒ University of Texas

2A ⓓ Vanderbyl Design ⓒ City of Richmond   2B ⓓ Hornall Anderson ⓒ Food Services of America

3A ⓓ Webster Design Associates Inc. ⓒ Strategic Air & Space Museum   3B ⓓ Dotzero Design ⓒ Star Advisors

ⓓ = Design Firm   ⓒ = Client

A

B

① = Design Firm ⓒ = Client

1A ① Gardner Design ⓒ Wichita River Festival 1B ① Wages Design ⓒ Chick-fil-A University
2A ① Gardner Design ⓒ Precision Datacom 2B ① Chermayeff & Geismar Inc. ⓒ Multicanal
3A ① Vanderbyl Design ⓒ US Air Force 3B ① Beth Singer Design ⓒ The American Israel Public Affairs Committee

1

2

3

1

BENEFITAMERICA

2

RANCH PARTY

3

1A ⓓ Chermayeff & Geismar Inc. ⓒ The American Film Institute 1B ⓓ Monigle Associates Inc. ⓒ EmployeeLife

2A ⓓ Device ⓒ Plan B 2B ⓓ Howalt Design Studio, Inc. ⓒ Phillip-Morris

3A ⓓ John Silver ⓒ Durban Cigars 3B ⓓ Felixsockwell.com ⓒ Target

ⓓ = Design Firm ⓒ = Client

A

B

D = Design Firm   **C** = Client

1A **D** Prejean LoBue **C** Mandalay Bay Resort & Casino   1B **D** Kellum McClain Inc. **C** The Actors Fund

2A **D** Prejean LoBue **C** Hagale Industries   2B **D** John Evans Design **C** Tejas Grill

3A **D** Sibley Peteet Design **C** Lone Star Donuts, Saunders, Lubinski & White   3B **D** Liska + Associates Communication Design **C** Stepping Stone Foundation

1

coral reef boutique

2

3

Stepping Stone Foundation®
PEDIATRIC NETWORK

A

B

1

2

LINKS FOR LIFE

SAN FRANCISCO FOOD BANK
Feeding the programs that feed the people

3

1A **D** James Lienhart Design **C** Congregational Church of Glen Ellen 1B **D** Device **C** Kill Your Boyfriend
2A **D** James Lienhart Design **C** James Lienhart Design 2B **D** McMillian Design **C** Golf Digest Magazine
3A **D** Addis **C** SF Food Bank 3B **D** Prejean LoBue **C** HCA Medical Center of Plano

D = Design Firm   **C** = Client

293

A

B

1

2

3

1A **D** James Lienhart Design **C** Chicago 27 Designers   1B **D** Cato Purnell Partners **C** Deep Fire Productions

2A **D** Wages Design **C** Atlanta Gas Light   2B **D** Cato Purnell Partners **C** Melbourne Olympics Committee

3A **D** Cato Purnell Partners **C** Westar Energy   3B **D** Wages Design **C** Georgia State University

A

B

1

2

3

1A Ⓓ Cato Purnell Partners Ⓒ Metasource 1B Ⓓ Howalt Design Studio, Inc. Ⓒ Phillip-Morris
2A Ⓓ Chase Design Group Ⓒ Crave Entertainment 2B Ⓓ Mires Ⓒ Gary's Rod and Custom
3A Ⓓ BrandEquity Ⓒ Dana-Farber Cancer Institute 3B Ⓓ Design and Image Ⓒ Sage

Ⓓ = Design Firm   Ⓒ = Client

A

B

D = Design Firm   **C** = Client

1A **D** Gardner Design **C** Catholic Stewardship Foundation   1B **D** Beth Singer Design **C** U.S. Department of Education
2A **D** Sayles Graphic Design, Inc. **C** HBO Films   2B **D** Chase Design Group **C** Hot Mustard Records
3A **D** Sabingrafik, Inc. **C** Tamasari Beverage   3B **D** Art Chantry **C** Hell's Elevator Prod.

1

2

3

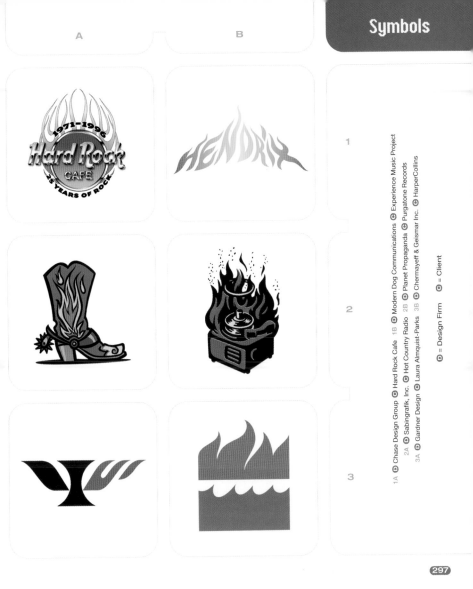

A

B

1

2

3

1A ⒹChase Design Group ⒼHard Rock Cafe 1B ⒹModern Dog Communications ⒼExperience Music Project
2A ⒹSabingrafik, Inc. ⒼHot Country Radio 2B ⒹPlanet Propaganda ⒼPurgatone Records
3A ⒹGardner Design ⒼLaura Almquist-Parks 3B ⒹChermayeff & Geismar Inc. ⒼHarperCollins

Ⓓ = Design Firm   Ⓒ = Client

Symbols

A

B

A

B

1

2

3

FEAA
FACULTATEA DE ECONOMIE
ŞI ADMINISTRAREA AFACERILOR

National
Children's
Literacy
Project

THE BLACK BOOK

1A ⓓ Grapefruit Design ⓒ Universitatea "Al. I. Cuza" Iasi, Romania   1B ⓓ Dotzero Design ⓒ Learning.com
2A ⓓ Hess Design Works ⓒ Lisa Palmer   2B ⓓ Liska + Associates Communication Design ⓒ The Black Book
3A ⓓ Evenson Design Group ⓒ California Literacy   3B ⓓ Dotzero Design ⓒ Literacy Volunteers

ⓓ = Design Firm   ⓒ = Client

A

B

1

2

3

D = Design Firm   **C** = Client

1A **D** Flynn Design **C** First Presbyterian Church   1B **D** Modern Dog Communications **C** www.1000journals.com

2A **D** Enterprise IG **C** Aurora Foods   2B **D** Sabingrafik, Inc. **C** Seaport Village

3A **D** Corporate Image Consultants Inc. **C** Manna Ministries   3B **D** Mires **C** The Yellow Pages

A

B

1

2

3

1A **D** Jon Flaming Design **C** Linda Lux Photography 1B **D** Gardner Design **C** Chauncey Photography

2A **D** Howalt Design Studio, Inc. **C** California Real Estate Magazine 2B **D** Jon Flaming Design **C** Party Pix

3A **D** Proart Graphics/Gabriel Kalach **C** Fotopianet 3B **D** Hornall Anderson **C** PhotoWorks

D = Design Firm   **C** = Client

A

B

⊙ = Design Firm   ⊙ = Client

1A ⊙ Sayles Graphic Design, Inc. ⊙ Big Daddy Photography 1B ⊙ Made on Earth ⊙ Iwerks
2A ⊙ Proart Graphics/Gabriel Kalach ⊙ Fotopia 2B ⊙ Hornall Anderson ⊙ Corbis Corporation
3A ⊙ Hoyne Design ⊙ Cinimagic 3B ⊙ Chase Design Group ⊙ Turner Pictures

A

B

1

2

3

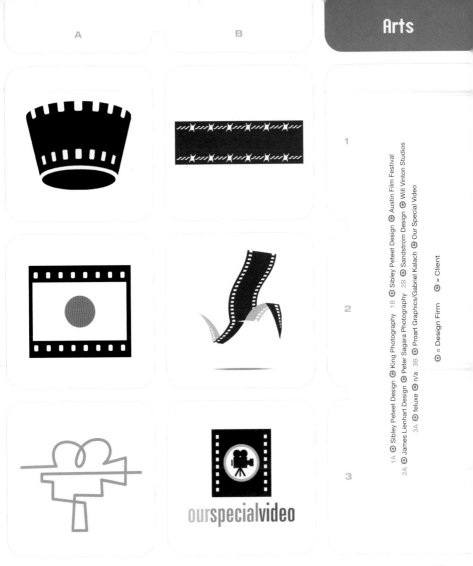

ourspecialvideo

1A ⒟ Sibley Peteet Design ⒞ King Photography 1B ⒟ Sibley Peteet Design ⒞ Austin Film Festival
2A ⒟ James Lienhart Design ⒞ Peter Sagara Photography 2B ⒟ Sandstrom Design ⒞ Will Vinton Studios
3A ⒟ feluxe ⒞ n/a 3B ⒟ Proart Graphics/Gabriel Kalach ⒞ Our Special Video

⒟ = Design Firm   ⒞ = Client

A   **B**

1

2

3

D = Design Firm   **C** = Client

1A **D** McMillian Design **C** Ken Coit   1B **C** Sabingrafik, Inc. **C** Oliver McMillin

2A **D** Proart Graphics/Gabriel Kalach **C** Our Special Video   2B **D** Braue; Branding & Corporate Design **C** Starke Veranstaltungen

3A **D** Gardner Design **C** AIGA Wichita   3B **D** Evenson Design Group **C** Radio Gabby

KC·VIDEO
DESIGN+PRODUCTION

SCREENLAND

ourspecialvideo.com

STARKE
VERANSTALTUNGEN

1

2

3

1A ⑩ Chase Design Group ⓒ The WB   1B ⑩ Cincodemayo ⓒ TMD Services

2A ⑩ Liska + Associates Communication Design ⓒ Expand Beyond   2B ⑩ Richards Brock Miller Mitchell & Associates ⓒ 1-800-AUTHORS

3A ⑩ Howalt Design Studio, Inc. ⓒ Ogilvy & Mather   3B ⑩ Cincodemayo ⓒ Telenet

⑩ = Design Firm   ⓒ = Client

A

B

1

2

3

Ⓓ = Design Firm   Ⓒ = Client

1A Ⓓ Be Design Ⓒ Microsoft 1B Ⓓ 2b1a Ⓒ Coffein Music

2A Ⓓ Evenson Design Group Ⓒ Rubin Postaer 2B Ⓓ Sabingrafik, Inc. Ⓒ Douglas Wilson Companies

3A Ⓓ Hoyne Design Ⓒ Triple J 3B Ⓓ Design and Image Ⓒ Colorado Symphony

A   B

1

2

3

1A ⑩ Felixsockwell.com ⓒ EW   1B ⑩ Design and Image ⓒ Cowtown Catering
2A ⑩ Visible Ink Design ⓒ Snake Music   2B ⑩ Prejean LoBue ⓒ Drew Morrison
3A ⑩ Howalt Design Studio, Inc. ⓒ Hard Drive   3B ⑩ Felixsockwell.com ⓒ EW

⑩ = Design Firm   ⓒ = Client

A

B

1

2

3

Ⓓ = Design Firm   Ⓒ = Client

1A Ⓓ Art Chantry Ⓒ Stereolab   1B Ⓓ Felixsockwell.com Ⓒ Creo

2A Ⓓ Felixsockwell.com Ⓒ Creo   2B Ⓓ Chermayeff & Geismar Inc. Ⓒ Graphic Arts USA

3A Ⓓ Howalt Design Studio, Inc. Ⓒ Howalt Design Studio   3B Ⓓ Prejean LoBue Ⓒ Prejean LoBue

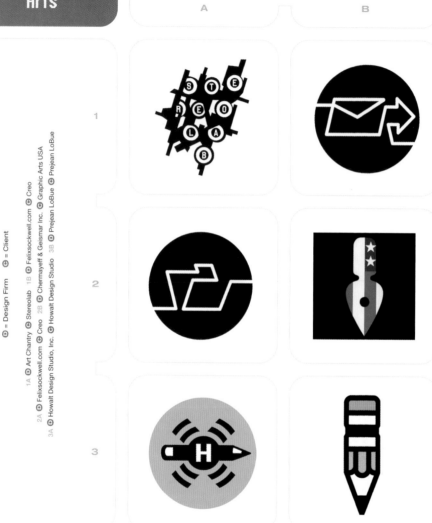

A

B

1

2

3

1A ⓓ Rickabaugh Graphics ⓒ Invisible Ink   1B ⓓ Trickett & Webb ⓒ London Institute

2A ⓓ Sabingrafik, Inc. ⓒ Design Safari   2B ⓓ Tharp Did It ⓒ The Design Conference That Just Happens To Be In Park City

3A ⓓ Felixsockwell.com ⓒ Creo   3B ⓓ Gardner Design ⓒ Amber Lear

ⓓ = Design Firm   ⓒ = Client

A

B

1

2

3

⊕ = Design Firm ⊖ = Client

1A ⊕ Jeff Fisher LogoMotives ⊖ Jeff Maul 1B ⊕ Felixsockwell.com ⊖ Creo

2A ⊕ Howalt Design Studio, Inc. ⊖ Herman Miller 2B ⊕ After Hours Creative ⊖ The Chair Academy

3A ⊕ Design One ⊖ Drexel Heritage 3B ⊕ Sayles Graphic Design, Inc. ⊖ Christine's 20th Century Design

A

B

1A ⓓ Made on Earth ⓒ Next Media 1B ⓓ Howalt Design Studio, Inc. ⓒ AT&T

2A ⓓ Saturn Flyer ⓒ KRYPTOSIMA 2B ⓓ feluxe ⓒ Creo

3A ⓓ Art Chantry ⓒ The 3B 3B ⓓ Gardner Design ⓒ DeCotiis Erhard Consulting

ⓓ = Design Firm   ⓒ = Client

A

B

1

2

3

1A **C** Prejean LoBue **C** Motorola   1B **D** Prejean LoBue **C** A Helping Hand

2A **D** Modern Dog Communications **C** Jackson Remodeling   2B **D** Art Chantry **C** Black Dog Forge

3A **D** Felixsockwell.com **C** Blackfoot Indian Construction   3B **D** Gardner Design **C** Brain Cramps

A

B

1

2

3

1A Ⓓ The Makers 1B Ⓓ Hornall Anderson Ⓒ Personify

2A Ⓓ Pure Imagination Studios Ⓒ Pure Imagination Studios 2B Ⓓ Hornall Anderson Ⓒ CW Gourmet/Mondeo

3A Ⓓ Made on Earth Ⓒ Made on Earth 3B Ⓓ Modern Dog Communications Ⓒ All The Rave, Inc.

1A Ⓓ Art Chantry Ⓒ The Makers

Ⓓ = Design Firm   Ⓒ = Client

Miscellaneous

	A	B

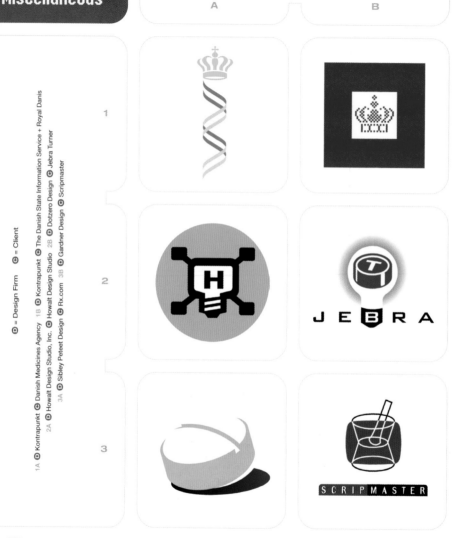

1

2

3

1A **D** Kontrapunkt **C** Danish Medicines Agency 1B **D** Kontrapunkt **C** The Danish State Information Service + Royal Danis
2A **D** Howalt Design Studio, Inc. **C** Howalt Design Studio 2B **D** Dotzero Design **C** Jebra Turner
3A **D** Sibley Peteet Design **C** Rx.com 3B **D** Gardner Design **C** Scripmaster

D = Design Firm   **C** = Client

A

BIG BOWL
AN ASIAN CAFE

PARTNERS IN CARING

DONCASTER

SSPC Children's Center

B

RETROLINER

fig. F

E-JUNK

GIVE
PEACE
A
DANCE

1

2

3

1A **Ⓓ** Essex Two Incorporated **Ⓒ** Lettuce Entertainment   1B **Ⓓ** Howalt Design Studio, Inc.   **Ⓒ** Retroliner.com

2A **Ⓓ** Design One **Ⓒ** Doncaster   2B **Ⓓ** Howalt Design Studio, Inc.   **Ⓒ** None

3A **Ⓓ** Graves Fowler Associates **Ⓒ** Silver Spring Children's Center   3B **Ⓓ** Art Chantry **Ⓒ** Legs Against Arms

Ⓓ = Design Firm   **Ⓒ** = Client

Miscellaneous

A

B

1

2

3

ⓓ = Design Firm   ⓒ = Client

1A ⓓ Art Chantry ⓒ KPLOTRA   1B ⓓ Design Machine ⓒ 555 Gallery

2A ⓓ John Silver ⓒ FrameStars   2B ⓓ Cato Purnell Partners ⓒ Grand Hyatt Jakarta

3A ⓓ Liska + Associates Communication Design ⓒ HealthLink   3B ⓓ Wages Design ⓒ Quantum

A   B

1

2

3

FADICA

ANYTIME TICKETS

1A **D** Gardner Design **C** Intracare 1B **D** Graves Fowler Associates **C** Foundations and Donors Interested in Catholic Activities, Inc.
2A **D** James Lienhart Design **C** Junior Womens Association 2B **D** Richards Brock Miller Mitchell & Associates **C** Firehouse Ministries
3A **D** Boelts/Stratford Associates **C** Colorado Dance Festival 3B **D** Jeff Fisher LogoMotives **C** Triangle Productions!

D = Design Firm   **C** = Client

D = Design Firm   C = Client

1A D Kiku Obata & Company C Barnes & Noble 1B D Sayles Graphic Design, Inc. C Java Joes
2A D Lieber Cooper Associates C Swissotel - Chicago, Illinois 2B D Sabingrafik, Inc. C Boyds Coffee
3A D Sabingrafik, Inc. C IVAC Corporation 3B D MB Design C Walton Beverage

1

2

3

A   B   **Food**

1

2

wineshopper   grape finds

3

1A Ⓓ Eisenberg and Associates Ⓒ Silver Spur Ranch 1B Ⓓ Prejean LoBue Ⓒ Regional AIDS Interfaith Network

2A Ⓓ Howalt Design Studio, Inc. Ⓒ Robert Mondavi 2B Ⓓ Hornall Anderson Ⓒ Grapefinds

3A Ⓓ Dotzero Design Ⓒ Bridgetown Printing 3B Ⓓ Trickett & Webb Ⓒ Rennies

Ⓓ = Design Firm   Ⓒ = Client

319

◉ = Design Firm   ◎ = Client

1A ◉ Art Chantry ◎ The Nomads   1B ◉ Gardner Design ◎ Applewood Grill
2A ◉ Dan Stiles Design ◎ Arjuna Veervagu (DJ Juice)   2B ◉ Sibley Peteet Design ◎ O's Catering
3A ◉ Sibley Peteet Design ◎ Chili's   3B ◉ Willoughby Design Group ◎ Lee Jeans

A

B

1

2

3

1A **D** Sayles Graphic Design, Inc. **C** Vino Viccino's   1B **D** Simon & Goetz Design **C** Sylvia Gellman
2A **D** Willoughby Design Group **C** Einstein Bros. Bagels   2B **D** Howalt Design Studio, Inc. **C** Wellsteads
3A **D** Dogstar **C** Typhoon Restaurant   3B **D** Lexicon Graphix, Inc. **C** The Stoop

D = Design Firm   **C** = Client

D = Design Firm   **C** = Client

1A **D** Dogstar **C** Jimmie Hale Mission   1B **D** Felixsockwell.com **C** la Bicyclette
2A **D** Cato Purnell Partners **C** National Museum of Australia   2B **D** Mitre Design **C** Opie's Southbound Grille
3A **D** feluxe **C** Firehouse   3B **D** Gardner Design **C** Fidel Bistro

A

B

1

2

3

1A ⓓ Chase Design Group ⓒ Tommy Stoilkovich 1B ⓓ Gardner Design ⓒ Excel Corporation
2A ⓓ Rickabaugh Graphics ⓒ Kernel Encore 2B ⓓ Randy Mosher Design ⓒ Brewsters Coffee
3A ⓓ Felixsockwell.com ⓒ Sure Fire 3B ⓓ Modern Dog Communications ⓒ Tidemark

ⓓ = Design Firm   ⓒ = Client

D = Design Firm   **C** = Client

1A **D** Hornall Anderson **C** Italia Restaurant & Wine Bar 1B **D** Gardner Design **C** Windowsill Foods
2A **D** Tim Frame **C** Charley's Steakery 2B **D** Tim Frame **C** Bob Evans Restaurants
3A **D** Willoughby Design Group **C** Noodles & Company 3B **D** Design and Image **C** Diane's

A

B

1

2

3

1A ⒟ AdamsMorioka Inc. ⒞ Disney ClubHouse   1B ⒟ Gardner Design ⒞ Hearth and Home
2A ⒟ Design and Image ⒞ Meridian Homes   2B ⒟ Prejean LoBue ⒞ Hearthscape Partners LLC
3A ⒟ Hecht Design ⒞ Transition House   3B ⒟ Felixsockwell.com ⒞ Ourhouse.com

⒟ = Design Firm   ⒞ = Client

Structures

A

B

D = Design Firm **C** = Client

1A **D** Richards Brock Miller Mitchell & Associates **C** The Family Place 1B **D** Gardner Design **C** Comfort Care Homes
2A **D** Phinney/Bischoff Design House **C** Seattle Housing Authority 2B **D** James Lienhart Design **C** City House
3A **D** Enterprise IG **C** Scienda 3B **D** Braue; Branding & Corporate Design **C** Druckhaus Wüst

1

2

3

PorchLight

Scienda™
Building Sciences

DRUCKHAUS WÜST

A B

1

2

3

1A ⓓ Gardner Design ⓒ Prairie State Bank 1B ⓓ Chermayeff & Geismar Inc. ⓒ Preservation League of New York State
2A ⓓ Pat Taylor Inc. ⓒ Type House (hot metal days) 2B ⓓ Associated Advertising Agency, Inc. ⓒ Energy Home Systems
3A ⓓ Jon Flaming Design ⓒ Lennox 3B ⓓ Sabingrafik, Inc. ⓒ People Movers

PEOPLE MOVERS

ⓓ = Design Firm   ⓒ = Client

Structures

Ⓓ = Design Firm   Ⓒ = Client

1A Ⓓ Sayles Graphic Design, Inc. Ⓒ Homeworks 1B Ⓓ MB Design Ⓒ Kulshan Community Land Trust
2A Ⓓ Howalt Design Studio, Inc. Ⓒ Janene Brown 2B Ⓓ Sabingrafik, Inc. Ⓒ Sea Country Homes
3A Ⓓ Sabingrafik, Inc. Ⓒ McMillin Homes 3B Ⓓ Essex Two Incorporated Ⓒ Burack & Company

1

2

3

1A ⒟ Mitre Design ⒞ Winston-Salem Downtown Arts District 1B ⒞ Balance ⒞ Inn at the Market

2A ⒟ Mires ⒞ Portcullis Management 2B ⒟ Roman Design ⒞ Fortress Technologies, Inc.

3A ⒟ Mitre Design ⒞ St. Paul's Episcopal Church 3B ⒟ Kiku Obata & Company ⒞ Simon Property Group

⒟ = Design Firm   ⒞ = Client

A

B

1

2

3

D = Design Firm   C = Client

1A D Tim Frame C Axis Group 1B D Art Chantry C Pitch & Groove

2A D Jon Flaming Design C Max Barney 2B D Jon Flaming Design C Central & Southwest

3A D Chase Design Group C The Paltrow Group 3B D Hornall Anderson C Space Needle

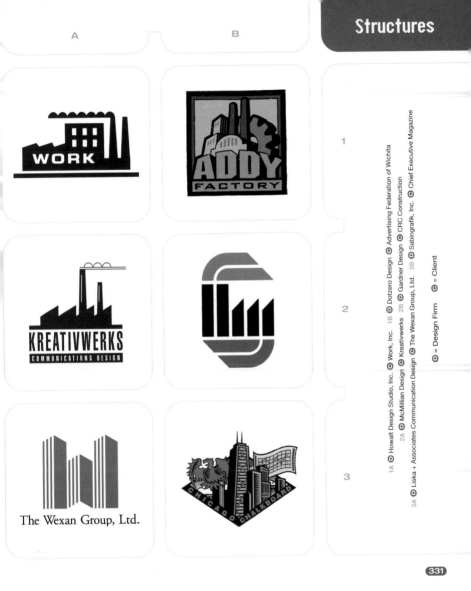

WORK

ADDY FACTORY

KREATIVWERKS
COMMUNICATIONS DESIGN

The Wexan Group, Ltd.

CHICAGO CHALKBOARD

1A ⓓ Howalt Design Studio, Inc. ⓒ Work, Inc.   1B ⓓ Dotzero Design ⓒ Advertising Federation of Wichita
2A ⓓ McMillian Design ⓒ Kreativwerks   2B ⓓ Gardner Design ⓒ CRC Construction
3A ⓓ Liska + Associates Communication Design ⓒ The Wexan Group, Ltd.   3B ⓓ Sabingrafik, Inc. ⓒ Chief Executive Magazine

ⓓ = Design Firm   ⓒ = Client

Structures

A

B

1

2

3

HANOVER ERLICH
REAL ESTATE

METROPOLIS

SHINING CITY
RECORDS

UPTOWN
CARWASH

Urban Market
DEVELOPMENT

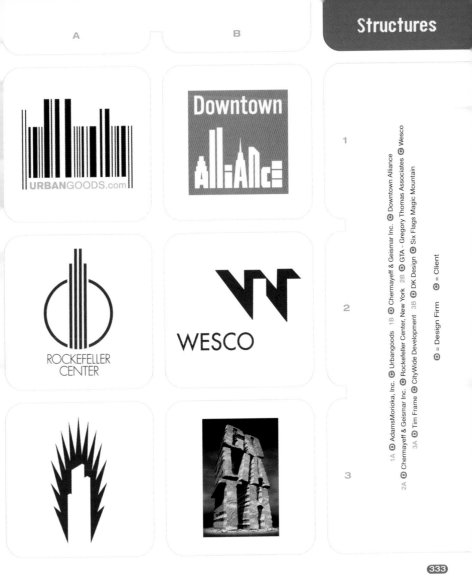

A

B

1

2

3

URBANGOODS.com

Downtown
AlliANcE

ROCKEFELLER
CENTER

WESCO

1A **D** AdamsMorioka, Inc. **C** Urbangoods   1B **D** Chermayeff & Geismar Inc.   **C** Downtown Alliance

2A **D** Chermayeff & Geismar Inc.   **C** Rockefeller Center, New York   2B **D** GTA - Gregory Thomas Associates   **C** Wesco

3A **D** Tim Frame   **C** CityWide Development   3B **D** DK Design   **C** Six Flags Magic Mountain

D = Design Firm   **C** = Client

A

B

THE DESIGN
MUSEUM
of FORM &
FUNCTION

RAFN

H. BEALE
COMPANY

CONCO
CONSTRUCTION

A   B   1   2   3

1A **D** Essex Two Incorporated **C** Horwitz-Matthews   1B **D** Hornall Anderson **C** RAFN Construction

2A **D** Pat Taylor Inc. **C** Hastings Development Corp.   2B **D** Jon Flaming Design **C** Jim Flaming

3A **D** Bird Design **C** H. Beale Company   3B **D** Gardner Design **C** Conco Construction

D = Design Firm   **C** = Client

Structures

A

B

1

2

3

A

B

1

2

3

1A **D** Corporate Image Consultants, Inc. **C** Walt Disney 1B **D** Sabingrafik, Inc. **C** Seaport Village

2A **D** Sabingrafik, Inc. **C** Seaus Restaurant 2B **D** Dogstar **C** Fog City Press

3A **D** Graves Fowler Associates **C** Fannie Mae 3B **D** Sabingrafik, Inc. **C** Ivac Medical Systems

D = Design Firm **C** = Client

Transportation

A   B

A

B

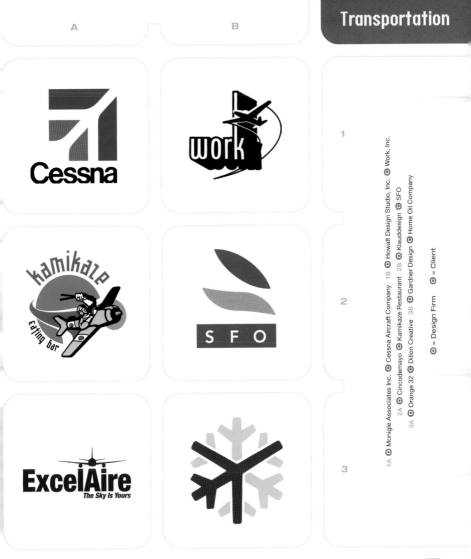

1

2

3

1A ⓓ Monigle Associates Inc. ⓒ Cessna Aircraft Company   1B ⓓ Howalt Design Studio, Inc. ⓒ Work, Inc.

2A ⓓ Cincodemayo ⓒ Kamikaze Restaurant   2B ⓓ Klauddesign ⓒ SFO

3A ⓓ Orange 32 ⓒ Dillon Creative   3B ⓓ Gardner Design ⓒ Home Oil Company

ⓓ = Design Firm   ⓒ = Client

A

B

D = Design Firm   **C** = Client

1A **D** Jon Flaming Design **C** Objex   1B **D** Hornall Anderson **C** Travel Services of America
2A **D** Klauddesign **C** SFO   2B **D** Buz Design Group **C** Nissan Motor Company
3A **D** Wages Design **C** Arris   3B **D** Dotzero Design **C** Mostella Records

1A ⓓ Made on Earth ⓒ Made on Earth 1B ⓓ Sabingrafik, Inc. ⓒ Cub Scout Troop 260
2A ⓓ Howalt Design Studio, Inc. ⓒ 12XU records 2B ⓓ Art Chantry ⓒ Estrus Records
3A ⓓ Sabingrafik, Inc. ⓒ California Beach Co. 3B ⓓ Howalt Design Studio, Inc. ⓒ CSA Archive

ⓓ = Design Firm ⓒ = Client

Transportation

D = Design Firm   **C** = Client

1A **D** Howalt Design Studio, Inc. **C** Prestone   1B **D** Sabingrafik, Inc. **C** Shimano Resort
2A **D** Art Chantry **C** Moe Wrecking Crew   2B **D** Art Chantry **C** Moe Putting
3A **D** Sayles Graphic Design, Inc. **C** Beckley Imports   3B **D** Jon Flaming Design **C** Greyhound

1

2

3

A

B

1

2

3

WORK INC.

WORK

THE ORIGINAL
dashboard

1A ⒟ Howalt Design Studio, Inc. ⒞ Work, Inc.   1B ⒟ Prejean LoBue ⒞ Old El Paso
2A ⒟ Howalt Design Studio, Inc. ⒞ Work, Inc.   2B ⒟ Cato Purnell Partners ⒞ Progressive Enterprises
3A ⒟ Cato Purnell Partners ⒞ Progressive Enterprises   3B ⒟ Tharp Did It ⒞ Dashboard

⒟ = Design Firm   ⒞ = Client

Transportation

A

B

1

2

3

D = Design Firm   **C** = Client

1A **D** Felixsockwell.com **C** Mikes Bikes   1B **D** Howalt Design Studio, Inc. **C** Calvary Church
2A **D** Gardner Design **C** Allens Excavating   2B **D** Dogstar **C** Heavy Talent
3A **D** Tim Frame **C** Anchor Manufacturing   3B **D** Chermayeff & Geismar Inc. **C** Anchor Engraving

A

B

1

2

3

1A **D** Wages Design **C** Yacht Haven 1B **D** Mitre Design **C** Snug Harbor Specialties

2A **D** Sabingrafik, Inc. **C** Deleo Clay Tile Company 2B **D** MB Design **C** Sails Aloft

3A **D** Hornall Anderson **C** Kirk Perron 3B **D** Sabingrafik, Inc. **C** Continental I - Trimaran Cruises

D = Design Firm **C** = Client

A

B

D = Design Firm   **C** = Client

1A **D** Sabingrafik, Inc. **C** Brightwater   1B **D** Hoyne Design **C** Fosters Group

2A **D** Kellum McClain Inc. **C** Crossroads Communications   2B **D** Sabingrafik, Inc. **C** South Shore

3A **D** Bright Strategic Design **C** Holland America   3B **D** Sabingrafik, Inc. **C** Harcourt Brace & Co.

1

Brightwater

2

3

A

B

1

2

3

1A ⒟ Sabingrafik, Inc. ⒞ McMillin Homes 1B ⒟ Wages Design ⒞ Lake Lanier Islands

2A ⒟ Evenson Design Group ⒞ Streamline Graphics 2B ⒟ Sabingrafik, Inc. ⒞ Alliance Federal Credit Union

3A ⒟ Lexicon Graphix, Inc. ⒞ Ironwood Technologies 3B ⒟ Design and Image ⒞ Union Station Paver Program

⒟ = Design Firm   ⒞ = Client

index

directory

2b1a
Germany
49.17.51.96.83.79

AdamsMorioka, Inc.
United States
310.246.5758
www.adamsmorioka.com

Addis
United States
510.704.7500
www.addis.com

After Hours Creative
United States
602.275.5200

Angryporcupine
United States
408.873.9021
www.angryporcupine.com

Art Chantry
United States
314.773.9421

Artimana
Spain
34.93.207.53.56
www.artinet.net

Artomat Design
United States
206.623.9294
www.artomatdesign.com

**Associated Advertising
Agency, Inc.**
United States
www.associatedadv.com

Balance
United States
830.990.2888
www.studiobalance.com

BBK Studio
United States
616.459.4444
www.bbkstudio.com

Be Design
United States
415.451.3530
www.beplanet.com

Luce Beaulieu
Canada
514.849.9075

Bel Bare
Australia
61.0413.459.610
www.belbare.com

Beth Singer Design
United States
www.bethsingerdesign.com

Bird Design
United States
616.458.4844
www.birddesign.com

Blue Beetle Design
Singapore
65.323.3282
www.bluebeetledesign.com

Boelts/Stratford Associates
United States
520.792.1026
www.boelts-stratford.com

BrandEquity
United States
617.969.3150 x232
www.brandequity.com

**Braue; Branding &
Corporate Design**
Germany
49.0471.983.82.0
www.braue.info

Brian Sooy & Co.
United States
440.322.5142
www.briansooyco.com

Bright Strategic Design
United States
310.305.2565
www.brightdesign.com

Bumba Design
United States
818.761.1353

Buz Design Group
United States
310.202.0140
www.buzdesign.com

Cato Purnell Partners
Australia
61.3.9429.6577
www.cato.com.au

Chase Design Group
United States
323.668.1055
www.margochase.com

Chermayeff & Geismar, Inc.
United States
212.532.4499
www.cgnyc.com

Cincodemayo
Mexico
52.818.342.5242
www.cincodemayo.com.mx

**Corporate Image
Consultants, Inc.**
United States
813.963.6729
www.cibydesign.com

CRE8 Communications, Inc.
United States
612.227.0908
www.e-cre8.com

Cronan Group
United States
510.923.9755
www.cronan.com

Dan Stiles Design
United States
415.720.3262
www.danstiles.com

Dennis Purcell Design
United States
310.301.0106
www.dennispurcelldesign.com

Design and Image
United States
303.292.3455
www.d-and-i.com

Design Machine
United States
212.982.4289
www.designmachine.net

Design One
United States
828.254.7898
www.d1inc.com

Device
United Kingdom
44.20.7221.9580

DK Design
United States
818.763.9448

Dogstar
United States
205.591.2275

Dotzero Design
United States
503.892.9262
www.dotzerodesign.com

Eisenberg and Associates
United States
214.528.5990
www.eisenberg-inc.com

Elixir Design
United States
415.834.0300
www.elixirdesign.com

Enterprise IG
United States
415.391.9070
www.enterpriseig.com

Essex Two Inc.
United States
773.489.1400
www.sx2.com

Evenson Design Group
United States
310.204.1995

Felixsockwell.com (feluxe)
United States
212.579.5617
www.felixsockwell.com

Flynn Design
United States
601.969.6448

Gardner Design
United States
316.691.8808
www.gardnerdesign.com

Grapefruit Design
Romania
40.232.233068
www.grapefruitdesign.com

Graves Fowler Associates
United States
301.816.0097
www.gravesfowler.com

GTA - Gregory Thomas Associates
United States
310.315.2192
www.gtabrands.com

Hecht Design
United States
781.643.1988
www.hechtdesign.com

Henderson Bromstead Art Company
United States
336.748.1364
www.hendersonbromstead.com

Hess Design Works
United States
914.232.5870
www.hessdesignworks.com

Hornall Anderson
United States
206.467.5800
www.hadw.com

Howalt Design Studio, Inc.
United States
480.558.0390
www.howaltdesign.com

Hoyne Design
Australia
61.3.9537.1822
www.hoyne.com.au

Hutchinson Associates, Inc.
United States
312.455.9191

Indicia Design, Inc.
United States
913.269.5801
www.indiciadesign.com

James Lienhart Design
United States
312.738.2200
www.lienhartdesign.com

Jeff Fisher LogoMotives
United States
503.283.8673
www.jfisherlogomotives.com

John Evans Design
United States
214.954.1044

Jon Flaming Design
United States
214.987.6500

Kellum McClain Inc.
United States
212.979.2661
www.kellummcclain.com

Ken Shafer Design
United States
206.223.7337
www.kenshaferdesign.com

Kiku Obata & Company
United States
314.361.3110
www.kikuobata.com

Klauddesign
United States
415.781.6021
www.klaud.com

Kontrapunkt
Denmark
45.33.93.18.83
www.kontrapunkt.dk

Laura Manthey Design
United States

Richard Leland
United States
443.604.3420
www.leland.nu

Lexicon Graphix, Inc.
United States
315.423.0510
www.lexicongraphix.com

Lieber Cooper Associates
United States
312.527.0800
www.liebercooper.com

**Liska + Associates
Communication Design**
United States
312.644.4400
www.liska.com

Logoboom
United States
323.650.6513
www.logoboom.com

Made on Earth
United States
818.761.4545
www.madeonearthstore.com

Marcus Lee Design
Australia
61.03.9429.3100
www.marcusleedesign.com.au

MB Design
United States
360.733.1692
www.mb-design.com

McMillian Design
United States
212.665.0043
www.mcmilliandesign.com

MetaDesign
United States
www.metadesign.com

Miaso Design
United States
773.862.5822
www.miasodesign.com

**Minale Tattersfield
& Partners Ltd.**
United Kingdom
44.0.20.8948.7999
www.mintat.co.uk

Mires
United States
619.234.6631
www.miresbrands.com

Miriello Grafico, Inc.
United States
619.234.1124
www.miriellografico.com

Mitre Design
United States
336.722.3635
www.mitredesign.com

Modern Dog Communications
United States
206.789.7667
www.moderndog.com

Mojo Unlimited, LLC
United States
www.mojounlimited.com

Monigle Associates Inc.
United States
303.388.9358
www.monigle.com

Orange 32
United States
631.864.0082
www.orange32.com

Pat Taylor Inc.
United States
202.338.0962

**Phinney/Bischoff Design
House**
United States
206.322.3484
www.pbdh.com

Planet Propaganda
United States
608.256.0000
www.planetpropaganda.com

Plumbline Studios
United States
www.plumbline.com

Pogon
Yugoslavia
381.11.626.039

Portal 7 Design
United States
212.254.4236

Prejean LoBue
United States
337.593.9051
www.prejeanlobue.com

**Proart Graphics/Gabriel
Kalach**
United States
305.532.2336

Pure Imagination Studios
United States
630.933.8167
www.pureimagination.com

Randy Mosher Design
United States
773.973.0240
www.randymosherdesign.com

Renegade Design
United States
330.899.0649

Richards Brock Miller Mitchell & Associates
United States
214.987.6500
www.rbmm.com

Rickabaugh Graphics
United States
614.337.2229

Rodgers Townsend
United States
314.436.9960
www.rodgerstownsend.com

Roman Design
United States
303.526.5740

S Design, Inc.
United States
www.sdesigninc.com

Sabingrafik, Inc.
United States
760.431.0439

Sackett Design
United States
415.929.4800
www.sackettdesign.com

Sandstrom Design
United States
503.248.9466
www.sandstromdesign.com

Sanna Design Group, Inc.
United States
516.719.6235
www.4sdg.com

Saturn Flyer
United States
571.212.0338
www.saturnflyer.com

Sayles Graphic Design, Inc.
United States
515.279.2922
www.saylesdesign.com

Sibley Peteet Design
United States
512.473.2333
www.spdaustin.com

John Silver
United States
425.379.8284
www.johnsilveronline.com

Simon & Goetz Design
Germany
49.69.96.88.55.0
www.simongoetz.de

SPATCHURST
Australia
61.2.9360.6755
www.spatchurst.com.au

Spiral Design Studio
United States
518.432.7976
www.spiraldesign.com

Spot Color Inc.
United States
703.378.9655
www.spotcolor.com

Start Design Ltd.
England
020.7269.0101
www.startdesign.com

Sterling Group
United States
www.sterlingbrands.com

Stone & Ward
United States
501.375.3003
www.stoneward.com

Studio Rayolux
United States
206.286.9963
www.rayolux.com

t.b.g. design
United States
770.474.6600
www.tbgdesign.com

Tharp Did It
United States

Tim Frame
United States
614.598.0113

Treehouse Design
United States
310.204.2009

Trickett & Webb
United Kingdom
44.0.20.7388.5832

Triple 888 Studios
Australia
61.2.9891.2888
www.triple888.com.au

Vanderbyl Design
United States
415.543.8447
www.vanderbyldesign.com

Visible Ink Design
Australia
61.3.9510.7455
www.visibleink.com.au

Wages Design
United States
404.876.0874
www.wagesdesign.com

Webster Design Associates Inc.
United States
402.551.0503
www.websterdesign.com

Willoughby Design Group
United States
816.561.4189
www.willoughbydesign.com

Woodhead International
Australia
61.8.8223.5013
www.woodhead.com.au

Zenarts Design Studio
United States
703.757.9551
www.tangled-web.com

about the authors

Catharine Fishel is a freelance writer who runs Catharine & Sons, an editorial company that specializes in working with and writing about designers and related industries. She is a contributing editor to *PRINT* magazine, editor of logolounge.com, and the author of many books, including *Paper Graphics*, *Minimal Graphics*, *Redesigning Identity*, *The Perfect Package*, *Designing for Children*, *The Power of Paper in Graphic Design*, *Inside the Business of Graphic Design*, *401 Design Meditations*, *How to Grow as a Graphic Designer*, and *LogoLounge 2*.

Bill Gardner is president of Gardner Design in Wichita, Kansas and has produced work for Bombardier/Learjet, Thermos, Nissan, Pepsi, Pizza Hut, Coleman Outdoor, Excel, Cargill Corporation, and the 2004 Athens Olympics. His work has been featured in *Communication Arts, Print, Graphis, New York Art Directors, Step By Step,* Mead Top 60, the Museum of Modern Art, and many other national and international design exhibitions. His works and writings regarding corporate identity and three-dimensional design have been published in numerous books and periodicals. Gardner has judged a number of design competitions nationally and internationally, including the *Communication Arts Design Annual.*